Lest We Forget

Lest We Forget

The Southam Men in The Great War

Alan Griffin

For my grandfather
Private Ralph Griffin
1st Battalion Bedfordshire Regiment
Killed in Action at Wulverghem
January 8th 1915

BREWIN BOOKS

First published in 2002 by
Brewin Books Limited, Doric House, Church Street,
Studley, Warwickshire B80 7LG

The author's moral right has been asserted.

British Library Cataloguing – in – Publication Data
A Catalogue record for this book is available from
The British Library

ISBN: 1 85858 216 4

Front Cover: A ration party of the Royal Irish Rilfes in a communication trench on the first day of the Battle of the Somme [IWM Q1)

Back Cover, Top: Mr J. T. Grant with family members home on leave.
Top Centre: The Battle of Pilckem Ridge 1917.
Bottom Centre: The Battle of the Somme, August 1916.
Bottom: Tommies group around a harmonium for hymn singing.

Made and printed by
Warwick Printing Company Limited,
Theatre Street, Warwick, Warwickshire CV34 4DR.

CONTENTS

ACKNOWLEDGEMENTS

My wife Lee has been the prime mover and principal encouragement in bringing this work to fruition. I readily acknowledge her help at every stage of the book's preparation. She shared with me many poignant moments in the vast cemeteries in Flanders wherein lie the remains of many of the young men mentioned in this book.

Robert Base provided invaluable assistance by locating and copying War Diary extracts in the Public Record Office at Kew. I am greatly indebted to him for his diligent and meticulous research on my behalf.

Having been told variously that the 19th Battalion Machine Gun Corps never served in the North Russia campaign and that there were no extant records of this unit at the PRO, I was both surprised and amazed to locate by means of the internet Martin Cassell. Martin has spent many years researching the Machine Gun Corps and is in possession of a double-sided sheet of typescript foolscap paper which comprises the original record kept by this company during its brief sojourn in Russia in 1919. The paper was given to him some twenty or more years ago by an MGC subaltern who had served there as part of the Syren Force.

My publisher Alan Brewin has my grateful thanks for helping aspiring authors such as myself to bring to publication works which are of essentially local interest and which would otherwise never have appeared in print. I thank him and his team most sincerely for their advice at every stage and for their expertise in producing a testament worthy of the men whose lives are here remembered.

Many people responded to my appeals for information and photographs and I offer particular thanks to the following individuals and organisations with apologies to anyone whose contributions may inadvertently have been overlooked.

Doris Amos, Peggy Bealing, Elizabeth Bishop, Irene Cardall & the Trustees of the Jack Cardall Collection, Martin Cassell, Eric Cleal, Ron Cleal, Hilda Eadon, George Fell, Mrs Gardner, Ken & Jacky Graham, Barry Grant, Bill Griffin, W. T. Griffin, Mr & Mrs Hancocks, Elaine Hancocks, Corinne Neale, Brian Parish, Edie & Ian Plummer, Norman Powell, June Sheasby, Gordon Shirley, Mrs Shorthouse, Marion Stanley, George Sturley, Rosemary & John Trussler, Dorothy Warner, Mary Williams, Richard Worrall.

Birmingham Reference Library
The British Library, Newspaper Library, Colindale
British Red Cross Society
The Commonwealth War Graves Commission, Maidenhead
In Flanders Fields Museum, Ypres
Imperial War Museum, Department of Printed Books
Imperial War Museum, Photographic Archive
Leamington Spa Library
Leicester County Record Office
Leicestershire Regiment Museum
Machine Gun Corps Research Group
Ministry of Defence, Personnel Records, Hayes
National Archives of Canada, Ottawa, Personnel Records Unit
Naval Historical Branch, Ministry of Defence
Office for National Statistics
Northamptonshire Regiment Museum
Royal Air Force Museum, Department of Research & Information Services
Royal Archives, Windsor Castle
The Royal Green Jackets Museum
Royal Navy Submarine Museum, Gosport
Royal Regiment of Fusiliers Museum
Royal Warwickshire Regiment Museum
Rugby Library
Shetland Sub Aqua Club
Warwickshire County Record Office
Warwickshire Yeomanry Museum
Western Front Association
Worcestershire Regiment Museum

AUTHOR'S NOTE

In a book aimed at a primarily lay readership and not presented as an academic work, it was felt that a plethora of footnotes/endnotes would serve no useful purpose and would impair somewhat its readability as a narrative. The principal sources consulted are listed over the page along with a select bibliography. The number of books dealing with all aspects of the Great War has burgeoned in recent years and a full list of all the works consulted would be impractical. I have included in the bibliography only those works which have a direct relevance to individual units or to particular actions and official reference works published by authority of the Government of the day. Also included is a short list of books which will be of interest to those who wish to undertake their own research into family members with Great War service connections.

I am happy to respond to written enquiries about anything referred to in the text and I welcome comments or information of any kind which can be forwarded to me via my publisher.

PRIMARY SOURCES

Unit War Diaries in the Public Record Office, Kew. WO95
Soldiers Service Papers in the Public Record Office (The 'burnt' documents) WO363
Soldiers Service Papers in the National Archives of Canada, Ottawa. RG150
The War Graves of the British Empire – Commonwealth War Graves Commission database (Now available on the internet)
Records of the Royal Aero Club, RAF Museum, Hendon
Casualty Records, Royal Flying Corps, RAF Museum, Hendon
Census returns for Southam – County Record Office, Warwick
Log Books for Southam Schools – Jack Cardall Museum
Southam Parish Magazine 1918 – 1922 – Southam Parish Church
Leamington Spa Courier newspaper 1914 – 1921 (On microfilm at Leamington library)
Rugby Advertiser newspaper 1914 – 1921 (On microfilm at Rugby library)
Warwick Advertiser newspaper 1914 – 1921 (On microfilm at CRO, Warwick)
Official History of the War – France & Belgium. Brig. Gen. Sir James Edmonds
British Regiments 1914 – 1918. Brig. E. A. James
History of the Great War – Order of Battle of Divisions. Ed. Becke
A record of the Battles & Engagements of the British Armies in France & Flanders 1914 – 1918. Capt E. A. James
Locations of British Cavalry, Infantry & Machine Gun Units 1914 – 1924. Robert W. Gould

Regiments and Corps of the British Army. Ian S. Hallows
Soldiers Died in the Great War 1914 – 1919. HMSO (Now available on CD rom)
Officers Died in the Great War 1914 – 1919. HMSO (Now available on CD rom)
British Battalions in France & Belgium 1914. Ray Westlake
British Battalions on The Somme. Ray Westlake
British Vessels Lost at Sea 1914 – 1918. HMSO

SECONDARY SOURCES

Allied Artillery of World War One. Ian V. Hogg
The 16th Foot: A History of the Bedfordshire & Hertfordshire Regiment. Major
    General Sir F. Maurice
*The 1st Battalion Dorsetshire Regiment in France & Belgium (August 1914 – June
    1915)*
Before Endeavours Fade. Rose E. B. Coombs
*Before the Echoes Die Away: The Story of a Warwickshire Territorial Gunner Regiment
    1892 – 1969.* N. D. G. James
*Birmingham Pals: A History of the three city Battalions raised in Birmingham in
    World War One.* Terry Carter
British Territorial Units 1914 – 1918. R. Westlake & M. Chappell
Christmas Truce: The Western Front December 1914. Brown & Seaton
The Day we Nearly Bombed Moscow. C. Dobson & J. Miller
Deeds that thrill the Empire. Hutchinson
The Forgotten Battles Series – Book Two Loos, 1915. Michael Gavaghan
Footprints of the 1/4th Leicestershire Regiment 1914 – 1918. J. Milne
For King & Country: The Canadians at Arras, August – September 1918. Norm
    Christie
For King & Empire: The Canadians at Vimy, April 1917. Norm Christie
*Gallant Canadians: The Story of the Tenth Canadian Infantry Battalion 1914 -
    1919.* Daniel G. Dancocks
The Hell they called High Wood. Terry Norman
Manchester Pals: A History of the two Manchester Brigades. Michael Stedman
Mons 1914. David Lomas
The Mons Star: The BEF 1914. David Ascoli
The Murmansk Venture. Maj. General C. Maynard
The Old Contemptibles. M. Barthorpe & P. Turner

The Oxfordshire Hussars in the Great War. Adrian Keith-Falconer
Seek Glory, Now Keep Glory: The story of the 1st battalion Royal Warwickshire Regiment 1914 – 1918. John Ashby
The Regional Military Histories: The Central Midlands. Lt. Col. Howard Green
Ships of the Royal Navy from the fifteenth century to the present. J. J. Colledge
The Somme: The Day-by-Day Account. Chris McCarthy
The Third Ypres – Passchendale: The Day-by-Day Account. Chris McCarthy
Three Before Breakfast: A true and dramatic account of how a German U-boat sank three British cruisers in one desperate hour. Alan Coles
The Warwickshire Yeomanry in the Great War. Hon. H. A. Adderley
When the Barrage Lifts. Gerald Gliddon
The Worcestershire Regiment in the Great War. Capt. H. Fitzmaurice Stacke.
Zeppelins Over England. Kenneth Poolman

FURTHER READING FOR RESEARCHERS

A Bibliography of Regimental Histories of the British Army. Compiled by Arthur S. White
Army Source Records of the First World War. Fowler et al (PRO Reader's Guides no 19)
Army Records for Family Historians. Fowler. (PRO Reader's Guides no 2)
RAF Records in the PRO. Fowler et al. (PRO Reader's Guides no 8)
The Location of British Army Records 1914 – 1918. Norman Holding
World War I Army Ancestry. Norman Holding
More Sources of World War I Ancestry. Norman Holding
Naval Records for Genealogists. N. A. M. Rodger
Battlefields of the First World War. Tonie & Valmai Holt
Death's Men; Soldiers of the Great War. Denis Winter
First World War. Martin Gilbert (the best paper back book on the war)
Kitchener's Army. Ray Westlake
Tommy Goes to War. Malcolm Brown
A Western Front Companion 1914 – 1918. John Laffin
The Western Front Illustrated 1914 – 1918. John Laffin
The Western Front. Richard Holmes
The World War One Source Book. Philip J. Haythornthwaite

The following poem was written in 1979 by Reg Paxton of the Southam branch of the British Legion and there is a framed version of it in the Lattey Chapel in Southam parish church close by the British Legion standards. I make no apology for taking the title of this book from Reg's poem and his daughter Sue has given me permission to reproduce the poem here.

Lest We Forget

Some gave their lives, and others met
With harm to mind and health,
So help is needed even yet
For most had little wealth.

Lest We Forget

They too were young – upon a time
And listened to the sound of Spring,
But then they fell in mud and grime
And for them, no birds sing.

Lest We Forget

They fought – and fight – just to ensure
That we can speak our mind,
So let us make life more secure
For loved-ones left behind.

Lest We Forget

Despite the help that others give
They need us even yet,
So please help, for those who live,
And show we don't forget

Lest We Forget

The author's grandfather Private Ralph Griffin served as a regular soldier before the war and is photographed in 1908 in the uniform of the Bedfordshire Regiment.

PREFACE

LEST WE FORGET – Alan Griffin

As a small boy I never quite understood why it was that my paternal grandfather had a different surname from my own. It was some years before I was able to resolve this childhood mystery to my satisfaction. As a Parish Church choirboy I had often stood shivering with my fellow choristers around the Southam War Memorial each Remembrance Sunday as the Rector read out the fifty or so names of those who had given their lives in the Great War. I must have heard the names read out on any number of occasions before I came to the realisation that 'R Griffin, Bedfordshire Regiment' was in fact my grandfather who had been killed in the war. My grandmother had remarried and my dilemma was resolved.

Having myself been born during the Second World War, there was little talk of the Great War when I was growing up in the nineteen fifties. What had previously been referred to as 'The Great War' had by then been relegated to just another historic conflict and had become 'The First World War'. It was as though more recent events had completely replaced in the public consciousness any remembrance of the events of 1914 – 18.

My mother's father had served in the Great War but seldom spoke about it or his part in it. His body bore mute but ample testimony to his experiences. In my grandparent's little two-up, two-down terraced house, there was no bathroom or indeed any running water in the house. My grandfather always used to shave in a bowl set up on the scrubbed pine table in the one downstairs room in which they cooked, ate and lived. As he stripped down to his vest and lathered up for his shave the lacerations on his arms and body were revealed to such of his close relatives who were permitted to witness this daily ritual. He had once confided 'I got wounded in the war', a comment which he chose never to elaborate on. That was as much as he ever said about being on the receiving end of machine gun bullets and red hot pieces of shrapnel.

For my grandfather the unspeakable horror of the Western Front was something that he himself had had to come to terms with. I suspect that for him and for many of his contemporaries the experience of war was too dreadful and harrowing to be recounted. It was in a quite literal sense unspeakable. Something to be locked away in the far recesses of the memory. A record of events that were almost surreal, a veritable hell into which ordinary God-fearing men were cast seemingly without prospect of redemption.

For most of my adult life I paid little regard to my grandfather's name carved on the Southam War Memorial. From time to time I used to stand for a few minutes beneath the memorial to read again the names and every time I stood there I was taken back thirty or forty years to those damp and blustery November afternoons of my childhood. I could still hear the Rector R. T. Murray reading out the names of the fallen. I heard again the young bugler Gerald Hall play *Last Post* and *Reveille*. I saw again frail old men with unsteady gait step forward somewhat hesitantly to place wreaths of red poppies against the names of men they had sat next to in Victorian school rooms. And at the going down of the sun on those late Autumn afternoons we all as one said that we would remember them. We **will** remember them.

The idea for this book was sown during one of those infrequent pilgrimages to the Southam War Memorial. It struck me just how little I knew about any of the men whose names had become familiar to me over the years. Who were they? What did they do in the war? How did they come to lose their lives? I knew that to try to answer many of these questions eighty or more years after their deaths would be something of a challenge. What I did not foresee was the tremendous emotional impact that would be made on me in the process of finding the answers. To visit the vast cemeteries and memorials along the Western Front and to lay a small cross on the grave of a Southam man you feel you know is both an intensely moving and a salutary experience. It is impossible not to be moved by the sheer scale of the slaughter and the grotesque waste of so many young lives. There were many times when I had to set aside the research and the writing simply in order to recover my emotional equilibrium.

I offer this book in the hope that it will serve as a fitting tribute to all of those Southam 'lads' known to us merely by their names who served and died in the world's first global conflict. Let it never be forgotten that they were all sons or husbands, fathers and brothers. Young men with the whole of their lives before them. It was their great misfortune to have been born in the closing years of the nineteenth century and on the eve of a war the likes of which had never before been witnessed. I hope that this modest work will in some small way illuminate their lives and the manner of their passing and in so doing may remind us of the huge debt of gratitude still owed to them at the start of the twenty first century.

Alan Griffin
Leamington Spa 2002

INTRODUCTION

On the eve of the Great War, Southam was in many respects an overgrown village with some of the features that might generally be associated with larger and more populous places. With a population of less than two thousand Southam was nevertheless one of Warwickshire's ancient market towns with a charter dating back some seven hundred years.

The town's heyday had passed along with the London stage coaches that once rattled into the cobbled yard of the Craven Arms hotel. The weekly corn market still functioned as did a monthly market for cattle but both were in a state of terminal decline. Opposition by many of the local landowners to the construction of railway lines in the parish had effectively sealed the fate of the once thriving livestock market and would seriously hamper the expansion of the town for many decades.

Save for the local cement and brick making industry, there was little employment in the district outside of agriculture and there was no major employer of any sort within the town itself. Perhaps surprisingly, the town supported a wide range of retail and commercial premises. There were five bakers and at least as many butchers and a dozen or so public houses and outdoor beer houses. Two mills operated in the town and branches of two of the major banks were long established. There were clock makers, boot makers, masons, tailors, lawyers, tin smiths and a number of grocers and small 'front room' sweet shops and general dealers. The town was self-sufficient in most respects.

Southam was the centre of a Poor Law Union and the imposing brick workhouse in Welsh Road had been built in early Victorian times to provide accommodation for 130 destitute men and women and the illegitimate children of single mothers. 'The Spike' also provided an overnight bed and a basic meal for the large number of vagrants who gathered outside the gates in the late afternoon each day.

There were separate schools for boys, girls and infants and the convent erected in the 1870's also provided free schooling for local children apart from the private tuition offered to the fee paying girls who lived in as boarders. It was never expected that children attending the convent school should be practising Roman Catholics, many children of other creeds received a first class education under the tutelage of the local nuns. A church building had been put up within the convent grounds and this was

XV

used by the town's expanding Roman Catholic community. A Congregational chapel in Wood Street and a Primitive Methodist chapel in Pendicke Street catered to the spiritual needs of non conformist worshippers and the Parish Church had an active congregation and a strong all male choir.

In common with towns and villages up and down the land, Edwardian Southam was host to a multitude of clubs, societies and sporting groups. It was this active participation of people in the life of the community and the sense of shared involvement which was the mortar that bound together the fabric of society in the days before the advent of cheap and accessible public transport.

Southam was a small enough place for folks to know who everyone else was and where they lived and frequently how they spent their lives. Little had changed there in the recent past. The Rector John Hart-Davies had held the living since 1895. Dr Walter Lattey had followed his father into the family medical practice in Wood Street and Joe Grosvenor had just retired after thirty six years at the Boys' School.

This then was Southam on the eve of the Great War. A small, close-knit and somewhat insular community where many families were inter related and where the curfew bell was still rung each evening as it had been for centuries past.

Many of the certainties that had underpinned life in this quiet rural backwater were about to be radically undermined by events in far off places on the other side of Europe.

Chapter One –

SAUCE FOR THE KAISER

The August Bank Holiday in 1914 fell on Monday August 3rd, a sweltering hot day in what had been one of the hottest summers in living memory. In the grounds of The Abbey in Leamington Road the local menfolk gathered to cast a critical eye over the exhibits for the annual Southam Flower Show. Like country folk everywhere they knew a thing or two about growing flowers and vegetables or at least they said they did!

In back yards and wash houses, the Southam women busied themselves folding their freshly boiled sheets and putting away the paraphernalia that formed part of the weekly ritual that was wash day. It had been a good drying day. As the copper fires were raked out and the heavy mangles were put away for another week, the womens' thoughts turned to a less mundane topic – the dance.

At The Abbey, the flowers and vegetables would soon be cleared from the large marquee ready for the evening dance on the lawn which always rounded off the day's festivities. Under the soft glow of oil lamps, the Southam folk sat down to enjoy a drink and as the Town Band struck up tunes suitable for dancing, the events of the day were again recounted.

Meanwhile, far away in London's Whitehall senior civil servants were poring over a large volume called the *War Book* in preparation for mobilisation. Great Britain and her Empire were but a few hours away from war with Germany.

As they danced away the balmy evening hours under the Abbey cypress trees, none could have imagined that their lives were about to be transformed in a most dramatic and ominous fashion. The lists of prizewinners still pinned up in the marquee bore the names of many young men who would never join the dance again. Before the Southam Flower Show came round once more, some would be crippled, some would be irreparably damaged in mind and body and many of them would be lying dead in unmarked graves in foreign lands.

By midnight on August 5th five empires were at war and several million soldiers were being hastily mobilised for a conflict which everyone confidently predicted would be over by Christmas. It had been almost a hundred years since a British army under Wellington had last fought a campaign in Europe. For much of the ensuing century, the profession of arms had been held in very low esteem particularly since the Boer War. Publicans frequently banned men in uniform from their premises and some even displayed signs reading 'No dogs – No soldiers'.

Despite the low opinion of the common soldier held by many people, young men were ever ready to take the King's shilling and to don a scarlet tunic for a life of travel and excitement. Three Southam men had died serving with the colours in the campaign against Russia in the Crimea in the 1850's. Others served in the South African wars and died at Ladysmith. There wasn't a lad in the town who didn't know about Troop Sgt. Major Seth Bond of the 11th Hussars who had taken part in the famous Charge of the Light Brigade at Balaclava and who lay buried in the churchyard.

Within a few hours, army form D463A (General Mobilization) dropped through the letter boxes of the small band of local men who had previously served in the armed forces and whose names were on the Reserve List for immediate recall in the event of hostilities. The form required the recipient to present himself for duty immediately taking with him his Identity Card, Life Certificate and his Soldier's Small Book. *The Warwick Advertiser* reported the names of those who had been summoned to defend their country's honour: F. Harrison, J. Checkley, R. Griffin, W. Baldwin, J. Fell and A. Waters. The men left without ceremony. No bands played. There were no formal farewells. Small knots of people gathered on Market Hill to wish the men 'God Speed' and a safe return. 'Come on Jack let's get it over with' was Ralph Griffin's wry comment as the two of them clambered into Joe Warwick's horse-drawn cab for the ride to Rugby railway station. Also mobilised were the local members of the Warwickshire Yeomanry, a county-based territorial cavalry unit. The Yeomanry mainly comprised men with farming and business backgrounds. The principal requirement was that all the men should be accomplished horse riders. The Southam Yeomen included Sergeant William Sturley, and Troopers Chambers, Sheasby, Shorthouse, Plummer, Neal and Smith.

A few miles away one of the British Army's most senior officers had also received his mobilisation orders. At Radway Grange in the shadow of Edge Hill General Douglas Haig had summoned his driver to convey him to Banbury to catch the fast train to London. The General's journey to the battle front began in a somewhat inauspicious manner. Despite repeated attempts by his chauffeur the staff car proved quite incapable of making the steep ascent of Sunrising Hill on the Banbury Road. After many unsuccessful charges at the slope the solution was found. The lowest gear on the vehicle was engaged – reverse gear! The car was turned round at the bottom of the hill and Haig sped up facing backwards with no doubt a certain loss of dignity. Douglas Haig set out that morning as Commander of 1 Corps of the British Expeditionary Force. When he returned from the war he would be a Field Marshall, Commander-in-Chief of the Army and in receipt of an Earldom.

At Osborne naval college on the Isle of Wight, young Alexander Lattey, the second son of Dr Lattey the Wood Street GP had just celebrated his seventeenth birthday with fellow naval cadets. The college was housed in the outbuildings and stables at Osborne House the former home of Queen Victoria then used as an annexe to the Royal Naval College at Dartmouth. Like many boys training for officership in the Royal Navy, Alexander Lattey had gone to Osborne straight from prep school and was already in his fourth year. At the outbreak of war, the senior term at Osborne, instead of being sent on to Dartmouth, were all sent to sea. On August 14th the young Lattey was gazetted midshipman and posted to *HMS Hawke* as *aide-de-camp* to the Captain Hugh P. E. T. Williams. It must have been a

A prewar postcard of HMS Hawke published by the Rotary Photo Company c.1908.

somewhat inauspicious appointment for a keen young lad of seventeen. *The Hawke* was a twenty year old cruiser which was in most respects obsolete. Three years earlier *Hawke* had been involved in a serious collision off Portsmouth with *RMS Olympic*, sister ship of the *Titanic*. Both vessels had been extensively damaged in the incident on September 20th 1911. Within a few days of his posting, Alexander Lattey and the crew on board *Hawke* were steaming out into the cold grey waters of the North Sea as part of the Northern Patrol.

In Southam, at her little cottage facing Abbey Green, Mrs Rathbone was busy removing all of her foodstuffs from the cupboard in the inglenook. Her little daughter Hilda looked on quizzically and when she enquired what her mother was doing was told 'We are hiding it from the Germans'. And so war came to Southam.

In London, Prime Minister Herbert Asquith had appointed Lord Kitchener as Secretary of State for War. Kitchener had been Commander-in-Chief of the British Forces during the Boer War and was a well known and popular figure at home. It was Kitchener's face that appeared on the now famous Army recruiting poster that launched a public appeal for 100,000 volunteers. Recruiting offices up and down the land were besieged by men wishing to enlist and in the capital mounted police were called out to control the huge crowds.

Within a few days, a Cabinet Committee on Food Supplies was established and maximum retail prices were fixed for many basic food items. The price of butter was to be held at 1s 6d per pound, granulated sugar would be fourpence ha'penny per pound and British bacon 1s 6d a pound. Local grocers formed District Committees to monitor supplies of foodstuffs and to regulate prices where possible.

The Courier reported the arrival in the district of Army representatives who had been sent to mark down horses suitable for service with the military. The huge increase in the numbers of those in uniform was matched by a similar increase in the number of horses required by the Army both as riding animals and for use as draught and pack horses. An infantry division required at least 5,500 horses to function effectively. The *War Book* provided for the requisitioning of 120,000 horses in the first two weeks of the war.

Rumours of spies led many people to cast a more than cursory glance at anyone who looked remotely like a foreigner. Two men with rucksacks on their backs arrived at Long Itchington one evening looking for lodgings and found that no one in the village would offer them accommodation. A rumour that the two men were German spies had preceded their every step. It turned out that the pair were artists on a sketching trip and they eventually found suitable lodgings in Stockton.

On August 12th the first troops of the British Expeditionary Force under Field Marshall Sir John French had landed in France. Over the next ten days, four infantry divisions and a cavalry division numbering some 100,000 men crossed the English Channel without the loss of a single man.

The largest component of the BEF was the reservist. Called back to the colours on mobilisation, reservists made up sixty per cent of the force sent to France and Belgium in August 1914. The problems of equipping a vastly increased army were considerable. Apart from the difficulties of providing each man with service dress, weapons and equipment, there were also serious shortages of horses for the artillery and cavalry. It soon became painfully obvious to the reservist infantryman that the stiff and frequently ill-fitting boots that he had been issued with were a source of great discomfort on the many marches along the unyielding French cobbled roads.

The arrival of the BEF at their various ports of disembarkation was greeted with tremendous enthusiasm by the local inhabitants. Ralph Griffin had rejoined his old regiment the 1st Battalion of the Bedfordshires and a regimental diarist tells how the Battalion marched through Le Havre headed by French Boy Scouts. Many of the men arrived at their Rest Camp minus buttons, badges and even caps, all eagerly requisitioned by local people desperate for a souvenir of some sort. The men were in high spirits, buoyed up by their rapturous welcome. There was a widespread feeling that right would soon prevail and that Tommy Atkins would bundle Fritz unceremoniously out of France and Belgium. Everybody knew that it would all be over by Christmas.

Within a week of landing in France units of the BEF found themselves close to the small Belgian town of Mons. Mons was the centre of a dreary industrial and coal mining area dotted with pit heads, slag heaps and small mining villages. On a stifling August Sunday morning as a thick mist lifted the BEF found themselves confronting a large force of German troops along the banks of the Mons – Condé canal. The combatants had stumbled on each other by chance. No less surprised were the local folk returning from church in their best Sunday clothes. Many of them were caught between the front lines of the opposing armies.

The first major clash of the war saw several Southam men involved in an action in which the infantry were outnumbered by three to one but the outcome of which came as something of a surprise to the Imperial

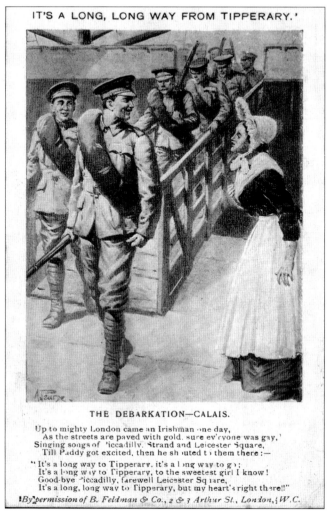

Men of the British Expeditionary Force disembarking at Calais in 1914.
A postcard published by Feldman & Co.

German Army. Mons was one of the few infantry battles of the Great War and it was the skill and training of Britains' small professional army that carried the day. Every BEF rifleman had been trained in musketry and his marksmanship was far and away superior to that of his German adversary. Every BEF man had been trained on the range for the so-called 'mad minute' during which he was required to get fifteen aimed shots into a two foot circle at a range of 300 yards. Many men could get off twenty-five aimed rounds a minute, a few could achieve thirty. The solid ranks of

German soldiers were met at Mons by a truly withering fire from the British positions. The intensity of the British rifle fire was such that the Germans thought they were being fired on by machine guns. In the thick of the fighting was Captain William Davidson in charge of 'D' company 1st Bn Dorsetshire Regiment. Davidson was the brother in law of Southam's Dr Lattey and uncle to the young midshipman Alexander Lattey on *HMS Hawke*. The Dorsets were holding a position to the right of the Bedfords, Ralph Griffin's regiment. Their diarist records how a large howitzer of 37 Battery parked alongside the Dorsets and fired at close range straight down a village street as though it were a machine gun. The rapid fire from the British Short Magazine Lee Enfield rifles made the barrels of some of them so hot that they couldn't be held. One of those present on the battlefield later wrote how 'The Germans went down like nine pins until we could see in front of us a regular wall of dead and wounded'. Another wrote home 'It was like a Third Division side playing the First Division'.

In spite of inflicting heavy losses on the German Army at Mons, the British Expeditionary Force found themselves in an untenable position. A series of independent withdrawals was ordered and so began a great retreat southward from Mons towards the French frontier. Another set-piece battle took place at Le Cateau on August 26th in an attempt to delay the pursuing Germans. In what turned out to be essentially an artillery engagement in open country, the hard pressed II Corps of the BEF were severely mauled. Official casualty figures show British losses of almost eight thousand men. Estimates of German losses varied from 15,000 to 30,000 dead.

What had started as a tactical retirement rapidly turned into the great Retreat from Mons. For the next two weeks the BEF men marched day and night almost a hundred and fifty miles. The Bedfords were to march 134 miles in just nine days. The reservists in particular suffered great distress on the march south. They were generally not as fit as the regulars and the stiff and ill-fitting army boots, the heavy serge service dress and the very hot weather combined to debilitate and exhaust even the fittest men. In field service marching order an infantryman carried over 60lbs (25kg) of equipment hung about his person. The scarcity of hot food and the snatched four hours sleep in a roadside field each night served to compound the men's discomfort. They knew that to have fallen out or collapsed by the wayside must have meant certain capture by the Germans. In the first week of September, the BEF crossed the river Marne and the Retreat from Mons ended.

Back home, the columns of the *The Leamington Spa Courier* were filled with the names of local men who had volunteered for service at the front and those of the National Reserve who were willing to re-engage for the war. Among those who lent cars to convey the Southam men to Warwick and Budbrooke Barracks to enlist were Dr Lattey and Captain Edward Davidson, the brother of William serving with the Dorsets. A meeting of the Red Cross Society was held in the Court House to enrol members for first aid and nursing duties and to discuss the setting up of a local Ambulance Corps. News of large numbers of horses being dispatched to the war front was also carried in *The Courier* which reported over a hundred horses being sent from Kineton during the last week of August.

The tremendous influx of recruits into the Warwickshire Yeomanry led to its ranks being many times over subscribed within a month of the declaration of hostilities. A waiting list of four hundred names of men willing to serve with the Yeomanry was soon posted and further recruiting was stopped. The latest draft of Yeomanry recruits entrained from Warwick station amid scenes of great enthusiasm *en route* to join the rest of the regiment in camp at Newbury. Some men had prepared large printed notices which were stuck on carriage windows proclaiming 'Warwickshire Sauce for the Kaiser' and 'First Stop – Berlin'. These sentiments typified the generally held view that this little difficulty across the channel would soon be sorted out once Tommy and his mates arrived.

Troopers and mounts of the Warwickshire Yeomanry in camp at Warwick Castle Park c.1912. George Shorthouse is the man fifth from the right.

Miss Irwin from The Lodge in Warwick Road paid a visit to the Girls School to exhort the children to collect eggs for wounded soldiers. Many of the girls were occupied during school time making garments for Queen Mary's Guild and for Belgian refugee children who were to be housed in the district.

On the fiftieth day of the war the first telegram was delivered in the town with news of a life laid down. The news was not of a death in the trenches of Flanders but of a drowning in the cold featureless wastes of the North Sea. Frederick William Court was serving as a Chief Armourer aboard *HMS Aboukir* when at 06.20 on the morning of Tuesday September 22nd 1914 she was torpedoed and sunk by submarine *U9*. The first torpedo fired in wartime had sunk the British light cruiser *HMS Pathfinder* in the Firth of Forth only two weeks before. The threat posed by German submarines had yet to be fully appreciated in Whitehall.

Aboukir formed part of the 7th Cruiser Squadron tasked to patrol a sea area known as the Broad Fourteens just off the Belgian coast and only 150 miles from the German naval base at Wilhelmshaven. The four cruisers

The sinking of the three cruisers in October 1914 was widely publicised by German propagandists. This German postcard from Her Majesty the Queen's collection shows HMS Aboukir almost totally submerged with the Hogue having just been struck amidships.

making up the 7th Cruiser Squadron *Aboukir, Bacchante, Cressy* and *Hogue* were obsolete four-funnelled ships which had been dragged out of a rusting retirement in the reserve fleet. *Aboukir* had been launched in 1900. At 12,000 tons apiece these armoured cruisers were cumbersome and although designed for a top speed in excess of 21 knots they were rarely capable of achieving better than 10 knots.

None of the look-outs in *HMS Aboukir* saw the torpedo's wake. It struck the cruiser behind the first funnel between the first and second boiler rooms and ripped out the bowels of the ship from the keel to the upper deck. Within a few minutes *Aboukir* was floating upside down and sinking, having got away only one boat, the cutter. On board the submarine, Oberleutnant Spiess the Watch Officer peered through the periscope trying hard to suppress his emotions as the drowning men fought to cling to the upturned lifeboats. The boat's Commander Lt Otto Weddigen later gave his account of the attack:

> *I had taken the position of the three ships before submerging, and I succeeded in getting another flash through my periscope before I began action. I soon reached what I regarded as a good shooting position. Then I loosed one of my torpedoes at the middle ship. I was then about twelve feet under water, and got the shot off in good shape, my men handling the boat as if she had been a skiff. I climbed to the surface to get a sight through my tube of the effect, and discovered that the shot had gone straight and true, striking the ship, which later learned was the Aboukir, under one of her magazines, which in exploding helped the torpedo's work of destruction. There was a fountain of water, a burst of smoke, a flash of fire, and part of the cruiser rose in the air. Then I heard a roar and felt reverberations sent through the water by the detonation. She had broken apart, and sank in a few minutes. Her crew were brave, and even with death staring them in the face kept to their posts, ready to handle their useless guns, for I submerged at once.*

Meantime a greater tragedy began to unfold as the other ships stopped and lowered their boats, the *Hogue* also throwing overboard mess tables and stools to assist the drowning men. While this work of rescue was in progress two torpedoes struck the *Hogue* and a further torpedo hit the *Cressy* which had all her boats away and mostly filled with survivors from the other ships.

Fifteen hundred British lives were lost in this single action, a death toll greater than at the Battle of Trafalgar. The majority of the sacrifices made on that morning were unnecessary. By some administrative oversight, no lifebelts had been issued when the ships' companies had joined at Chatham back in August. Many of the ships boats had been put ashore to provide more deck space. On that fateful September morning there were only eight serviceable and fully-manned lifeboats afloat in the North Sea. Between them they could hold barely a third of the men who floundered in the debris-strewn water.

Fred Court was probably a reservist, as were the larger proportion of the crews. He was 42 years old when he died. His wife Emily lived at the Gas House in Welsh Road and had given birth to a a son Fred at Southam on August 18th. A son that his father never saw.

As the warm sunshine of late Summer gave way to the cooler days of Autumn on the Western Front the early mobile phase of the war on land came to an end. From the French coast to the Alps the opposing armies now faced each other in hastily dug trenches and from behind breastworks of earth and stones raised up on the low-lying Flanders plain. Along the section of front line held by the BEF their forces invariably held the low-lying ground. The Germans had contrived from the outset to occupy any high ground which could be more readily defended and which over-looked the British positions.

Early on a morning thick with mist, the Germans began an artillery bombardment of Givenchy in the Arras sector which was held by the Bedfords and the Dorsets. The date was Tuesday October 13th. In the trenches with the 1st Bn Dorset Regiment was Captain W. T. C. Davidson in charge of 'D' company. The war diary of the Dorsets recorded the events of the day.

> *1.45pm. Oct 13th. Germans advanced from east end of Givenchy some carrying lances. About 250 suddenly appeared from the left rear of 'C' coy. These were mistaken for French Cavalry and fire was not opened on them. About a Battalion appeared about 900 yards from the left of 'C' coy. As soon as it was seen that these were Germans fire was opened on them. The Germans advanced holding up then either one or both hands. This was taken as a sign of surrender and some men left the trenches to go towards the Germans who then closed in rapidly driving in our men and enfilading the trench.*

The trench was deep and narrow and it was impossible for the Dorsets to get out quickly or mount any offensive action. An afternoon of bitter hand-to-hand fighting took place before the Dorsets were able to withdraw to a more tenable position. The Battalion suffered over 400 casualties as a result of this pretended surrender by German troops. Captain William

Davidson was killed leading his company. *The Courier* reported his death and his distinguished service through the South African Wars.

Young Midshipman Alexander Lattey aboard *HMS Hawke* would not have heard news of his uncle's death. His own thoughts would doubtless have been very much with his fellow naval cadets lost when *Aboukir* and her sister ships had gone down just over two weeks before. Ten young Midshipmen aged under fifteen had been among those drowned.

On the morning of October 15th *HMS Hawke* was cruising in the North Sea in line abreast, in company with four other cruisers of the 10th Cruiser Squadron. At 09.30 *Hawke* and *Endymion* were stopped and in the process of exchanging mails by cutter. *Hawke* hoisted aboard her boat and was proceeding at about 12 knots to regain her station when about 10.30 there was an explosion abreast the foremost funnel. The engines were stopped and almost immediately *Hawke* began to list. There was time to lower only the two sea boats, one of which was crushed by the ship which turned over and sank within minutes. Of the ships company of 400 only three officers and 49 men escaped. Midshipman Alexander Lattey was not among them. One of the survivors, a stoker recalled how those on board *Hawke* were enjoying themselves and singing songs when the ship was hit. "When I gained the upper deck the captain was on the bridge yelling to everyone to save himself. 'It's everyone for himself' he was yelling. I snatched a lifebelt and plunged over the rail to find myself with dozens of others who had done the same. I took little notice of how the others were getting on. There was not time. When I came up the *Hawke* was settling down and within four minutes she had disappeared." Among those who also lost their lives was another local man, Reuben Mann from Bishops Itchington one of *Hawke's* stokers.

What none of those on the North Sea on that Thursday morning knew was that *HMS Hawke* had been sunk by a torpedo from submarine *U9* commanded by Kapitan-Leutnant Weddigen, the very same combination that had sunk *Aboukir, Cressey* and *Hogue* only three weeks before.

Two telegrams arrived in quick succession at Hammerfest, Dr Lattey's house opposite the chapel in Wood Street. His brother-in-law and his youngest son, a mere lad of seventeen, had been killed within two days.

Mid-October brought with it a drawing in of the days and the chance for local lads to go 'conkering' under the large horse chestnut trees in the churchyard. The shortening Autumn days had for generations of Southam folk also been a timely reminder of the imminent arrival of the Mop Fair, always held on the first Monday after the twelfth of October. The Mop was always one of the 'big days' in the local calendar when an

Page 253

The War Illustrated, 31st October, 1914.

Germans Wildly Rejoice at Our Naval Losses

GERMANY went wild with delight over the sinking of the three British cruisers Aboukir, Hogue, and Cressy in September. The officer in command of Submarine U9, which did the damage, was Lieut-Capt. Otto Weddingen. He was married only a short time previous to setting forth on his daring exploit. In recounting his adventure, he praised the courage of the men on the British ships. "All the while," he said, "the men stayed at their guns looking for their invisible foe. They were brave; true to their country's sea traditions."

H.M.S. Hawke, an old cruiser of 7,350 tons and 19·5 knots, was sunk by a German submarine in the northern waters of the North Sea on October 15th. This was the ship which came into collision with the gigantic liner Olympic in 1911. Some of the crew rescued from the water are shown in the photograph above, and the cruiser is pictured on the left.

How the German submarine U9 was greeted when she returned to Wilhelmshaven, the great German naval base, in the early morning of September 23rd, after sinking three British cruisers. The officers and men of the submarine lined up on their vessel and received a wild ovation from the crews of German warships. The picture is by a well-known German artist.

This is a page from The War Illustrated, a part-work published during the Great War. It records the loss of HMS Hawke and the other ships sunk by submarine U9.

ox was roasted on Market Hill. Mabel Griffin's thoughts turned to the time when her Ralph had won the annual competition at the Mop for singing a song whilst holding a greasy pig under his arm. No Mop was held in Southam in the first year of the war, and few could have guessed that it would be many years before the showmen's gaudy wagons came their way again.

Across the channel, the BEF had moved north into Belgium, and the flat low-lying farmland of Flanders around the old mediaeval cloth town of Ypres. The allied front line bulged out to encircle Ypres forming what came to be known as the Ypres Salient. It had been decided that the British forces should attempt to outflank the Germans at Ypres. Instead of the planned offensive, the operation rapidly developed into a series of sometimes desperate defensive actions by the Allies in the First Battle of Ypres.

The 1st Battalion of the county regiment, the Royal Warwickshires were in trenches near to the village of Houpelines and under heavy artillery and sniper fire. The Battalion had earlier taken part in an attack on the village of Meteren but had been forced to withdraw due to lack of support and in the process suffering 246 casualties. Among the wounded was Lieutenant (later Field Marshall) B. L. Montgomery, seriously wounded when a bullet passed through his chest as he led his platoon. It was thought that he was mortally wounded and a grave had been dug. The Battalion diary for October 27th 1914 reported:-

> *Enemy shelled 'C' and 'D' companies trenches and sniped continuously and opened with maxims on them. Our guns shelled enemy's trenches and houses in vicinity. 6 killed, 15 wounded, all casualties from enfilade fire.*

This enfilade fire was the cause of a great many casualties during the early phases of the war. What it meant was that an enemy had positioned himself to shoot along the length of a trench from one or both ends; an extremely dangerous situation for those trying to defend the position. The snipers on both sides were exceptional marksmen. Frequently working in two-man teams of marksman/observer and equipped with binoculars or telescopic sights and high-powered rifles, the effects of sniping were devastating. Since the sniper's aim was at the victim's head, the shot was invariably fatal. Such was the fate that befell one of the original Southam reservists in the salient on October 27th. The Major's pencilled entry in the war diary on that date was to provide the epitaph for the first Southam reservist to lay down his life on the field of battle.

One of the six men killed on October 27th was Private 9671 John Checkley, one of those recalled to make up the Expeditionary Force. Born in Stockton, John Checkley had lived in Leamington Road, Southam at the outbreak of the war. He was the first of the town's fallen to be dignified by a proper burial and a grave marker. His body was laid to rest along with those of his colleagues in Strand Military Cemetery on the edge of Ploegsteert [Plugstreet] Wood. The cemetery was one of the first to be constructed to serve a Dressing Station at the end of 'The Strand', a trench which led into the wood.

The onset of Winter on the Western Front was heralded by periods of incessant rain and extreme cold. It would be one of the worst winters in living memory.

Across the battlefields of Flanders the BEF prepared themselves for their first Christmas of the war in the twenty one miles of rudimentary trenches that made up the British front line. In truth, these trenches were frequently little more than shallow ditches which were permanently

The primitive conditions in the trenches at the start of the war can be seen in this official photograph of the 2nd Battalion Royal Scots Fusiliers at La Boutillerie during the winter of 1914–1915. The men are wearing a variety of clothing and headgear to protect them from the cold. Rifles are positioned in loopholes made in the sandbags which face the enemy lines. [IWM Q49104]

flooded and impossible to keep dry. The water table was within two feet of the surface and any excavation quickly filled with water and thick slimy mud of porridge-like consistency in which men had to stand for days at a time. This constant immersion in freezing cold water caused feet to swell and become terribly inflamed, an extremely painful and debilitating condition which became known as 'trench foot'. The only way in which protection could be afforded from rifle and machine gun fire was by the construction of breast works built up with earth-filled sand bags stacked up like a wall in front of the trench. The trenches were not at this period connected to those in the rear of the line and had no protection from the elements. In these appalling conditions Battalions saw out their regular spells of front line duty.

First Ypres stuttered to an end in mid-November with the front line positions little changed. Ypres was still in the hands of the Allies but the fighting in the salient had wrought irreparable damage on the old professional British Army. When Regiments were mobilised for war little more than three months earlier, each Battalion mustered almost a thousand men. By the end of November there remained in each Battalion an average of just one officer and thirty men.

The first Battery of the Warwickshire Royal Horse Artillery landed in France in November and was the first Territorial artillery unit to enter active service in the war. The Battery was normally stationed at Clarendon Place in Leamington Spa and numbered Southam men among its ranks.

In Warwickshire, a major recruiting drive organised by the Motor Recruiting Service took place on a Sunday in late November. A convoy of 62 motor cars left Leamington Town Hall on a forty mile tour of local villages. In the cars were representatives of the local county Regiment, the Yeomanry and the Royal Horse Artillery, Army Service Corps and the Army Veterinary Corps. At each village on the route, the cars were halted and the men marched through the main streets headed by the Southam Town Band. When young men came out to see what all the commotion was they were accosted by energetic recruiting sergeants. The tour attracted a good deal of attention as it passed through Kineton, Southam and Long Itchington. In Southam *The Courier* reported that 'a touch of realism was added to the scene by a huge lorry from the War Department passing through the town on its way to Coventry with a disabled motor-car'.

The cost of the war was now running at a million pounds a day and the Chancellor of the Exchequer, Lloyd George announced a gigantic £350 million War Loan. He also announced a doubling of income tax to one and sixpence in the pound on earned income and increased the duties on beer and tea. "I am bound to assume" he said "that the war will be long".

One of those who had provided a car for the Recruiting Drive was Mrs Nellie Irwin from The Lodge in Warwick Road. Her late husband had been Vicar of Napton and her son Ronald was also in Holy Orders and serving as Chaplain to the Headquarters Staff (Meerut Division) of the Indian Expeditionary Force. In a letter to *The Daily Mail* a fellow officer described how Irwin was witness to the forced-landing of a German aeroplane near Locon where he happened to be talking to two soldiers. The article recounts how the 'local padre' captured the pilot and his observer who also had with them complete plans of the German trench systems in the area.

In Southam, the Red Cross Society continued to support the local men serving at the front. *The Courier* reported that fund-raising entertainments had been organised at the Convent and by Mr Grahame Hylton at the Southam Picturedrome. A large number of articles had been donated and sent off to benefit the troops including blankets, day and nightshirts, scarves, cholera belts and mittens and 103 pairs of socks. Thirty ladies including four Sisters from the Convent had received First Aid instruction from Dr Lattey and had successfully passed the examination.

With the approach of Christmas, there was much reflection on the state of a war that in earlier days everyone had confidently expected to be over by the year's end. In early December, collecting boxes were distributed to local pubs and shops to provide a Christmas parcel for each of the 104 Southam soldiers and sailors away at the war. By the middle of the month, the hundred and four parcels were ready for posting 'to cheer our Country's heroes at Christmastide'. *The Courier* reported that 'thirty parcels were despatched to the front, while the remainder were sent to quite a vast number of other destinations in practically all parts of the world'.

As the parcels were being carefully packed in Southam, on the Western Front the 2nd Battalion of the Royal Warwickshire Regiment was engaged in an unsuccessful and costly attack on the German lines near Bas Maisnil. The war diary records how the Battalion 'advanced with steadiness suffering heavy casualties'. The attackers were somewhat hampered by a flock of dead sheep that had lain out in No-Man's Land since the Autumn. Scores of the Warwickshires were hit by British shellfire which fell short of the German lines and the enemy positions were not taken. Many of those who managed to cross the 150 yards of No-Man's Land ended up hanging on the German barbed wire.

When the Battalion mustered back in the trenches after the action, only 149 men answered the roll call. The diary records 7 officers killed and 3 missing and 363 other ranks killed, wounded or missing. An informal armistice was called to enable both sides to remove the dead and wounded from the battlefield. Among those killed was the Warwickshire's new Commanding Officer Lieutenant-Colonel R.H.W. Brewis. He was the Battalion's second C.O. to be killed within two months. Of the scores of other ranks who were killed, one was a Southam man. Private Edwin Wellings was a native of Astley in Shropshire and a plasterer in civvy street. His wife Susan was six months pregnant when she received news at Christmas of her husband's death. Albert, the little lad that his father never saw was born in March the following year.

In Flanders,the wet weather of the Autumn and early Winter gave way to much colder and clearer conditions on Christmas Eve. After a frosty moonlit night, and a misty dawn, Christmas Day was bright and sunny. The many corpses still lying out in No-Man's Land were covered with a thick white rime. It would prove to be a day quite unlike any other day of the war. The men 'stood to' just before dawn as they did every day in anticipation of an enemy attack but in many sectors of the front line there was an uncanny silence. The sounds of carol singing drifted across No-Man's Land in the still, clear morning air. As the day wore on a widespread armistice became apparent. Men on both sides left the trenches and met to exchange greetings and to swap souvenirs and cigarettes. Photographs were taken and drinks were shared. On some sectors of the front impromptu games of football were played. The Cheshires killed and cooked a pig they had found behind their lines and shared it with the Germans. Up and down the line the dead of both sides were collected and brought in for burial in small regimental plots with simple and poignant services. For many men, the unaccustomed silence was an abiding memory of a quite extraordinary Christmas Day. A Private in the Royal Warwicks, wrote in his diary 'I miss the sounds of the shots flying over, it is like a clock which has topped ticking'.

The Christmas Truce was short-lived and the clock of attrition resumed its inexorable ticking on Boxing Day. The British High Command took a rather dim view of the widespread fraternization. General Sir Horace Smith-Dorrien issued a stern memorandum to the commanders of II Corps expressing his concern at the 'apathetic state we are sinking into' and instructing that 'on no account is intercourse to be allowed between the opposing troops'.

Chapter Two –

FIGHTING FOR CHRISTIAN PRINCIPLES

The turning of the year brought a return of the heavy rains and the Flanders trenches again turned into water-filled ditches. In Southam there was a heavy fall of snow and widespread flooding when a thaw set in. At the Horse & Jockey public house [The Old Mint] landlord William Langton and his daughter Polly were busy organising parcels of food and cigarettes to post to their 'regulars' serving in the war. One such parcel was destined for Private Ralph Griffin of the 1st Bn. of the Bedfordshire Regiment. The Bedfords had just gone back into trenches at Wulverghem to relieve the Dorset Regiment. The war diary records that

> *The trenches are in a very bad state, full of water, sides fallen in. We shot 2 enemy at close range who were moving along parapet of their communication trench; probably their trench was full of water. Our trenches and Germans' only about thirty yards apart in places.*

On Friday January 8th 1915 Ralph Griffin was shot through the head by a German sniper as he opened the parcel sent by his Southam pals. Ralph lived in Mountfield Gardens and was well known in the town. He worked for the Prudential Insurance Company as a local agent and was a regular worshipper at both the parish church and the Congregational Church in Wood Street. He was a church bell ringer and before the war had been captain of the Southam United Football Club first team. His young wife Mabel found herself a widow after less than four years of marriage. With a totally inadequate War Widows Pension, she took a job in a Midlands munitions factory in order to support her three small boys.

With little censorship in the early months of the war, local men wrote long and detailed letters to their loved ones back home describing conditions at the front and the actions in which they had taken part.

Many of these letters were passed on to local newspapers who were eager for any scrap of information about the progress of the war.

The *Rugby Advertiser* carried a letter from Tom Sheasby a Napton man who wrote 'I would not have missed this for a good deal as I have always wanted to get to a war'. A Coventry man wrote home on a paper serviette describing the Christmas Truce saying 'I dare say you will be surprised when I tell you that it contained a cake given to one of our men by a German officer on Christmas Day, and that I was given some of it'. Private Alf Day, another Napton man serving with the Royal Warwickshire Regiment also described the truce and said 'We should have played them [the Germans] at football if we had had a ball'. The high idealism and patriotism of the BEF men was much in evidence in the letters. Sam Taylor a Stockton man wrote 'We are fighting for what we believe to be Christian principles. We are fighting to keep the enemy away from England and our homes, and shall feel we have done our duty when victory is assured'.

On the night of January 19th the Germans carried out their first bombing raid on mainland Britain when two Zeppelins crossed the North Sea and dropped bombs on Great Yarmouth and Kings Lynn killing six civilians. In Southam, an outbreak of scarlet fever led to the closing of the infants school where half of the 93 children were sick.

His Majesty King George V leaves Dunchurch station with senior Army officers to review the 29th Division at Stretton On Dunsmore prior to their departure for Gallipoli in the Spring of 1915.

Great excitement was caused in Southam and much of east Warwickshire by the arrival in the district of large numbers of troops from the north of England and Scotland. The 2nd Field Company Royal Engineers, a territorial unit raised in Glasgow, arrived in Southam by train from Scotland. The *Rugby Advertiser* reported that good billets were found with local families for the 230 or so men who 'had not slept in beds for some time'. The Assembly Rooms in Warwick Road were placed at their disposal and games, books and other facilities were provided by a local committee chaired by Dr Lattey. The men were part of the 29th Division which assembled and mobilized early in 1915 in Warwickshire. The Divisional headquarters were in Leamington Spa. The 29th Division were reviewed by King George V at Stretton-on-Dunsmore before embarking for the uncertainties of a campaign in a new and previously unheard of theatre of war – Gallipoli. A name that would become synonymous with death and suffering on an awesome scale.

A group of mainly Scots soldiers make up this impromptu 'musical' group photographed outside the Dun Cow in Daventry Street in early 1915 when they were billeted in Southam for several weeks. The civilian (seated second from the left) is thought to be the pub landlord Ernie Owen who lost a son in the war.

The Southam column in the *Leamington Courier* carried a list of twenty five local footballers affiliated to the Leamington & District League who had joined the colours. The men were serving with twenty different units and ten of them were destined never to return from the war.

Throughout the early months of 1915, the British were quite unable to prosecute the war on their section of the Western Front in anything like a satisfactory way. The BEF was severely handicapped by an acute shortage of ammunition and particularly shells for the artillery. All the combatants had gone to war in the expectation of a short conflict and there had been no significant expansion of the production of artillery ammunition. By the end of February, the British 18 pounder field guns were restricted to firing just ten rounds a day. By the end of April, the situation had deteriorated further and they were down to a mere three rounds per gun each day. Apart from the shortages of ammunition, there were also serious shortages of uniforms and personal equipment and many of the Army items that came under the general heading of 'trench stores'.

There was an addition to the trappings of the front lines when barbed wire made its appearance. First manufactured in America in the 1870's it had been widely used by cattle ranchers to corral their livestock. On the Western Front it would serve to ensnare countless thousands of hapless men who could be fired on with impunity and at leisure.

Local men at the front continued to write graphic and descriptive letters to folks back home but the time would soon come when only the very vaguest of scripts would pass muster with the Battalion censor. Bill Burnell, a Southam-born man serving with the Royal Warwicks, wrote to his wife Jane at Stockton 'I think it will be a long war, and those who see the start and finish can shake hands with themselves'. In a letter written to his son he said 'I am still in the land of the living and after last week's affair it makes me think I am not to be shot'. He made an almost casual reference to having been blown off his feet by a high explosive shell that landed nearby and to 'one of the beggars' having made a bullet hole in his coat sleeve.

Walter Child of Holt Farm Southam serving with a Yeomanry regiment wrote to *The Courier* to report on his unit's participation in the Battle of Neuve Chapelle. He described how his 'best chum' Jack Brown from Cubbington was helping him to carry a heavy maxim gun. Having been ordered to withdraw from the front line trenches, they were negotiating a mile and a half of knee-deep mud when Child described how 'poor Jack had his brains blown out. Poor chap he never spoke. I was close to him and it made me feel sick for a bit but we got used to that. .... It was a grand week altogether. I would not have missed it for a good bit'. His letter ends with a reflection on the shortage of ammunition and an appeal to the paper's readers. 'How many more men have you got in Southam & district fit? Do not let them rest till they have joined. Take it from me every man is needed'.

The letters reflect the almost fatalistic attitude held by many men in the front line and the matter-of-fact way they came to terms with death. Walter Child returned to Southam at the end of hostilities. William Burnell's simple optimism was to be confounded however. He did not die from small arms fire but would be dead within a month, killed by an exploding shell.

The men of the Warwickshire Yeomanry had been in training at Norwich since December of 1914 and on April 10th 1915 embarked from Avonmouth for overseas service. The majority of the regiment left on *HMT Saturnia*, the Regiment's 763 horses and mules were put aboard the transport *Wayfarer* with 189 NCO's and men. Early on the afternoon of the following day the *Wayfarer* was torpedoed as the ship passed north west of the Scillies. A number of Southam Yeomen who were on board *Wayfarer* were picked up by the *Framfield* a passing steamer. Of the officers and men on board *Wayfarer*, only five lives were lost and all of the horses were taken safely ashore. The local newspapers reported that 'Three Southam Troopers Plummer, Sheasby and Shorthouse were aboard the liner when torpedoed, but all have written home to their parents to say they are safe'.

The Warwickshire Yeomanry eventually arrived in Alexandria in mid-May and received a number of letters of congratulation from army top brass including an Army Order issued by Lord Kitchener the Secretary of State for War. The GOC of the 2nd Mounted Division Major General W. E. Payton wrote to say that he felt sure that 'the record established on that occasion will cause all units to emulate their sense of discipline, their courage and their devotion to duty in the hour of danger, whenever and under whatever circumstances opportunity presents itself'. There was a certain irony in his remarks. The Yeomanry were to be torpedoed for a second time before the Armistice was signed.

In late April, the British took over 5 miles of former French front line to the north-east of Ypres and it was here on the afternoon of April 22nd that the Germans used poison gas for the first time. The Second Battle of Ypres cost the 1st Battalion of the Royal Warwicks over 500 casualties with 16 officers killed or missing.

Harry Askew from Leamington Road was serving in the salient with the 1st Bn of the Rifle Brigade. Their war diary records how the Battalion moved by train from billets near Ballieul to Poperinghe. When troops were conveyed by rail, they didn't travel in conventional railway carriages but in French cattle wagons marked '8 chevaux – 40 hommes' (8 horses or 40 men).

The Rifle Brigade detrained at Poperinghe and after two days marching reached hill 37 near Fortuin. Here they took over some large dugouts constructed and previously occupied by the French. This sector was thinly garrisoned and the diary records that the Battalion were not in contact with any other British units on their right flank. A platoon was sent out to try to establish which other units were in close proximity. At dawn on April 27th, the Germans opened up heavy shelling on the British positions and this continued day and night for the next two days. The war diary records 103 casualties on the 26th and 'about 60' on the following day. Harry Askew was one of those killed on April 27th.

Men of Harry Askew's Rifle Brigade Battalion photographed in Ploegsteert (Plugstreet) Wood during the Winter of 1914 – 1915. The harsh conditions showed up the serious deficiencies of clothing and coats and jerkins of sheepskin and goatskin were issued early in 1915. [Rifle Brigade Club]

Harry Askew enlisted at Winchester at the start of the war and had been posted to France in January 1915. He gave as his next of kin his brother Herbert then living in Banbury Road, and another brother Alfred in Jarrow on the river Tyne. Harry's remains were never recovered. His name is just one of over fifty five thousand carved on the Menin Gate at Ypres. This huge memorial archway stands astride the Menin road along which most of those whose names are carved on it would have passed on their way to the trenches. It commemorates all those allied soldiers who died in the salient up to 1917 and who have no known graves.

News of the death of another Southam man came within a few days. Ernest Davenport was an acting Corporal with the 2nd Bn. Royal Welsh Fusiliers. His father Edward was described in the 1891 census returns as a coal merchant in Daventry Street. In 1912 his name appeared in *Kelly's Directory* as a farmer in Stockton Road. The RWF were in the line near Armentieres, a fairly quiet sector of the front. Ernest Davenport was one of a small wiring party which had gone out at night into no man's land to strengthen the barbed wire in front of the British lines. Wiring was very much a job for skilled soldiers and was a particularly dangerous task. Wooden or steel pickets were taken out and placed in their selected positions under the guidance of NCO's. The pickets were then driven into the ground using large wooden mallets with their heads muffled with strips of old hessian sacking. The rolls of barbed wire were then attached and drawn out to form an apron on either side of the newly fixed posts. The task had to be carried out in the dark and in absolute silence. The slightest noise would betray the men's position and bring down a hail of small arms fire on the party. The Fusilier's war diary records that the Germans fired three short salvos on the Battalion's trenches on April 29th. The third salvo arrived at 9.30pm just as the wiring party were out in no man's land. Two of the men were killed and three injured by what must have been a purely speculative German salvo.

By the end of 1915, and for the first time in living memory, there was an acute shortage of labour on the land. George Smith who farmed at Holt Farm, Southam placed his property and all his livestock in the hands of a Banbury auctioneer. The Notice of Sale made clear his reason for giving up farming – his only son was joining His Majesty's Forces. Children were everywhere excused school to help with potato picking and the many labour-intensive jobs that went with agriculture. The Army Council allowed soldiers to help with work on the land and it wasn't long before a new kind of agricultural worker began to appear on local farms in the form of Land Girls.

At the start of the war, the Government had passed the Defence of the Realm Act (DORA) which came to regulate many aspects of people's lives at home. Further regulations were enacted as the months passed. Public houses were ordered to close during the morning and afternoon whereas before the war they had been open all day from early morning till late at night. Beer was watered down to reduce its potency and it became an offence to buy a round of drinks in a pub or to 'treat' a friend in a bar.

By May 1915, the first of the hundreds of thousands of men who had responded to Lord Kitchener's appeal for volunteers were trained and ready for active service overseas. The first of the so-called New Army divisions the 9th (Scottish) Division embarked on May 9th 1915. Two days earlier, a German submarine had sunk the Cunard liner *Lusitania* off the coast of Ireland with the loss of over 1,000 lives, an event which led to an explosion of anti-German sentiment in Britain.

On the Western Front, General Sir Douglas Haig was launching a major offensive at Festubert just north of the La Bassée canal. Here the objective was to take German lines about 1,000 yards away, the attack would be preceded by a 60-hour artillery bombardment. This operation would mark a new policy of attrition by the British on the Western Front. Henceforth, their declared intention would be to gradually wear down the enemy 'by exhaustion and loss until his defence collapses'.

Among the troops taking part in the attack on May 16th were members of the 2nd Battalion Royal Warwickshire Regiment. At first light, the Battalion formed up in company order in the British front line trenches ready to go over the top. German artillery opened a heavy bombardment of the front line and support trenches causing many casualties among the assembled Warwicks. The Battalion diarist records how the companies advanced across no man's land 'with great dash and quickness and arrived at (the) desired objective'. Unfortunately, the rest of the day did not go well for the Warwickshires. When they got into the German trenches they came under heavy enfilade fire and were forced to withdraw to their own lines. A day of confused fighting ensued with companies and platoons of the Warwicks being sent to support a number of Battalions who were under a determined German counter-attack. As the day wore on they provided reinforcements for the Royal Welsh Fusiliers, the Queen's and the Royal Scots. The diary speaks of 'troops unable to advance' and 'advanced British troops retiring'. During the night of May 17/18 the diary records that the battlefield was cleared and the dead buried. The entry concludes with a list of the names of officers killed and missing and a note indicating that two hundred 'other ranks' were killed, wounded or missing during the operation.

One of those killed was Private William Burnell. A friend wrote with details of his death. 'I expect Mrs Burnell has heard how her husband got killed. William Moore from Long Itchington was with him when it happened. A Jack Johnson [German shell that exploded with a lot of black smoke] burst against four of them and poor old Bill Burnell was amongst them. Me and Wally [Noon] and Bill Burnell were always together. I expect you know William Burnell, his nickname was 'Fatal'." Bill Burnell had been born and brought up in Southam where he had attended the Congregational church as a young man. He had married a Southam girl, Jane Pardington, and several of their children were christened in Southam parish church. He was another of the pre-war army regulars on the reserve list. His death left a grieving widow and eight fatherless children.

The Summer of 1915 saw the formation of a new all-party Government in Britain headed by Asquith and the appointment of Lloyd George as Minister of Munitions. The first step towards conscription came when all men between 18 and 41 were asked to 'attest' that they would enlist if called upon. Those who were above the upper age limit were to be allowed to serve as Special Constables.

Southam received news of the Scots engineers who had been billeted in the town earlier in the year. The news was not good. Many of the men were reported killed in action in Gallipoli. One of those killed was the Company Commander Major W. Archibald. Of the men who had been billeted in Long Itchington, *The Courier* reported that only a fifth of the 250 men were still in the fighting line against the Turks. 'The majority are either killed, or wounded or are suffering from sickness'.

Miss Irwin went to the Girl's School to thank the pupils who had decided to forego their prizes for the year, instead donating the money to the Southam Hospital Supply depot. A framed certificate was also presented to the school in recognition of the girl's efforts in collecting over 800 eggs for soldiers and sailors at the war. There were individual certificates for those who had collected 100 eggs. Over the road at the Boy's School, Mr Potton was granted a days holiday to travel to Rugby and Warwick in order to join the Army. He returned to school the next day to inform the headmaster that he had enlisted as a surveyor in the Rugby (Fortress) Company of the Royal Engineers and had to report for duty within 48 hours.

At the end of September, the Allies began a major offensive on the Western Front with the intention of relieving pressure on the Russians on the Eastern Front. On September 25th the British were to attack on a six-and-a-half mile front between Loos and Haines. This was a flat

Postcards performed a valuable morale-boosting role and were widely used during the war to promote causes associated with the welfare of men at the front. This card is in support of the National Egg Collection.

Men of the 2nd Battalion Royal Warwickshire Regiment being conveyed through Dickebusch to Ypres on London buses in November 1914. The first buses to be used on the Western Front arrived in their civilian colours but were later painted khaki and had their lower windows boarded up. Over six hundred buses ultimately operated organised by seven bus companies. [IWM Q57328] featureless mining area dominated by two large lattice-girder towers at a pit head known to the British Tommies as 'Tower Bridge'. For the first time in the war the British released large quantities of poisonous chlorine gas across no man's land prior to the infantry attack. One Battalion went over the top dribbling a football, the 15th (Scottish) Division walked through their own gas cloud led by a piper playing 'Scotland the Brave'. The day was wet and many of the infantry were thoroughly soaked having marched for several hours to arrive at the positions where they were to muster for the attack. As they crossed the half-mile of neutral ground to the German front lines in a series of short rushes, men gasped for breath in the primitive gas masks. They were greatly hindered by the mica eye-pieces misting up and obscuring their limited field of vision.

The early gas masks were little more than rudimentary face pads secured with thin straps as can be seen in this photograph of Argyll & Sutherland Highlanders taken in 1915. The design evolved over time into a hood-like helmet but the masks were still extremely uncomfortable to wear. [IWM Q48951]

Of the 10,000 British soldiers who went into action at Loos over 8,000 were killed or wounded. The Germans had early in the war been convinced of the effectiveness of the machine gun as a battlefield weapon and at Loos they were deployed in large numbers and to devastating effect. The advancing columns of British infantry were mown down in their thousands. German regimental diaries record whole Battalions of men being wiped out by traversing machine guns. The battle became known as Der Leichenfeld von Loos, the 'Field of Corpses of Loos.' The official history would later describe the first day at Loos as 'a day of tragedy, unmitigated by any gleam of success'.

Southam man Harry Brain was serving as a Sergeant with the 1st Battalion Royal Welsh Fusiliers. Together with the 2nd Queen's, 2nd Royal Warwicks and 1st South Staffs they made up the 22nd Brigade. Harry Brain was one of 442 casualties from his Battalion. He was killed when the Battalion was ordered forward to support 2nd Royal Warwicks who had been caught up in the German barbed wire which in many places was still uncut. Harry Brain had been born and christened in Southam and lived as a child in Abbey Row. He had attended the Congregational church as a lad and at the time of his death was living in Rugby. He was in all probability a reservist. His name is commemorated on the Loos Memorial to the Missing, his remains were never recovered.

There were other Southam men on the battlefield that September morning. Eric Lattey, brother of the young Midshipman drowned on the *Hawke* was serving as a Lieutenant with the 2nd Worcesters and was wounded at Loos. The Worcesters lost half their Battalion to rifle and machine gun fire. Like so many of the British offensives, the battle dragged on for several weeks before petering out in November.

By mid December, Sir John French the British Commander in Chief was given a title and removed from his command. His job as C-in-C went to General Douglas Haig a career soldier with local connections. At home the redoubtable Miss Irwin continued to organise a local collection for the National Egg Society and in one four-week period was able to dispatch the truly remarkable quantity of 2,321 eggs to the Society for the benefit of wounded combatants.

On the Western Front, it rained continuously throughout November. The trenches were in an appalling condition and most were knee-deep and some waist high in water. There was no fraternisation at Christmas 1915 and no repeat of the spontaneous truce of the first Christmas of the war. Many artillery batteries were ordered to maintain a slow gun fire on the enemy trenches from first light on Christmas Day. German troops at

Wulverghem set up a candle-lit Christmas tree above their front line trench on Christmas Eve. A burst of rapid fire from the British trenches soon extinguished the guttering candles and put paid to any thoughts of another armistice.

Local newspapers carried a message from the King appealing for 'men of all classes to come forward voluntarily and take your share in the fight'. To give 'support to our brothers, who, for long months, have nobly upheld Britain's past tradition, and the glory of her Arms". His Majesty had no doubt been briefed that come the new year, Lord Kitchener would be introducing conscription!

Chapter Three –

A WONDERFUL DISREGARD
FOR DEATH

It became clear that voluntary effort alone would not be sufficient to win the war. There was a widespread feeling that many single men who were fit for service had not volunteered while large numbers of married men had joined up and were serving at the front. The first week of 1916 saw the introduction of conscription. All single men between the ages of 18 and 41 were required to enlist for service. From May all married men would be conscripted. At Southam Boys' School Mr Barry left the school to enlist in one of the Irish Regiments.

The normal Saturday afternoon programme of league football became yet another casualty of the continuing hostilities. With large numbers of men away at the war, it became increasingly difficult for local teams to field a side. For many folks living in country districts, the local games of football were one of the few accessible forms of popular entertainment. It was not uncommon for local 'derby' games to attract over a thousand fiercely partisan spectators. Neither was it unheard of for elderly ladies to invade the pitch wielding brollies to belabour the poor unfortunate referee on those occasions when his decisions did not meet with popular approval.

Another Southam soldier died early in the new year. Hubert Pearson was a sapper serving in France with the 82nd Field Company Royal Engineers. He died of wounds on January 14th and is buried in the Communal Cemetery at Merville. Little is known about Hubert Pearson. He gave his address as Evesham Road, Astwood Bank in Worcestershire. Records suggest that he was born in Southam and his name is one of those on the Memorial Tablet in the Congregational Church which commemorates former members of the church and Sunday School who fell in the war.

As the war dragged on, the civilian population at home came under enemy fire for the first time. After the bombardment of some east coast towns by German cruisers earlier in the war, a new and sinister war machine entered the arena. With the deployment of the Zeppelin airship, the German High Command had the capability to bomb British cites from the air almost at will. Flying at night and at a height of over six thousand feet, they presented a quite serious threat and in early 1916 a number of raids were experienced over the Midlands.

The threat of Zeppelin raids caused considerable disquiet in Warwickshire. The Chief Constable of Leamington warned that he would prosecute anyone who failed to comply with the Lighting Restriction Order. He also ordered the cessation of the chiming of all public clocks during the night. The public were urged that 'when an alarm is given of a raid and the town is plunged into darkness, everybody should go home, and there should be no parading of the central thoroughfares to see what is happening'. It was perhaps unfortunate that no one had yet worked out quite how the general public were to be given warning of an impending attack!

The Southam Volunteer Fire Brigade was ordered to stand by in anticipation of a Zeppelin raid on the evening of March 6th 1916. The men donned their melton tunics and passed the night in the engine house in Pendicke Street boiling water for their cocoa on the pot-bellied stove. Bedworth had the doubtful distinction of being the target of a bomb dropped by a Zeppelin and although Warwickshire suffered little from the raids, nationwide fourteen hundred people were killed in over a hundred raids throughout the war.

After a spell of unseasonal spring-like weather in February, the last week in March saw severe gales and blizzards sweep across the Midlands. *The Courier* reported heavy losses of sheep and lambs on Southam farms and of livestock having to be dug out of six and seven feet of snow. It was reported that 219 telegraph poles had been blown down on the Banbury Road between Southam and Farnborough and that telegraph and telephone services were completely disrupted. Members of the Volunteer Defence Corps were engaged for several days helping to remove fallen poles and trees from local roads.

At Leamington Town Hall a number of local shopkeepers were fined 15 shillings each (75 pence) for allowing lights to shine from business premises with inadequate blackout. George Clarke a Stratford chauffeur was fined a similar amount for showing two bright side lights on a motor car in Willes Terrace. He told the Mayor that he wasn't aware that there were any lighting regulations in force. Also before the Leamington Bench was a hapless man aged thirty nine from Barratt Place in the town. Having been remanded in custody on a charge of attempting suicide by cutting his throat with a pen knife, he was told the charge would be withdrawn if he agreed to enlist.

At Easter, newspapers at home were filled with news from Ireland where in Dublin there was a full-scale rebellion against British rule. News from the war continued to be heavily censored and the Asquith Government decided that in future no casualty figures would be released.

By this stage of the war, a large number of troops had been sent from all parts of the Empire to support the British and French on the Western Front. The Canadians had committed 150,000 men, all volunteers, since the outbreak of the war and before the armistice would have half-a-million men under arms. Many of those who enlisted in the Canadian Expeditionary Force were quite recent emigrants from England. A number of Southam men had gone out to Canada before the war. They little expected that within a matter of months they would be heading back across the Atlantic in troop ships to fight and die in places they had never heard of.

The 18 pounder seen here at Montauban in July 1916 was the standard British Field Gun of the Great War and was generally close behind and sometimes in the line to provide close-support for the infantry. The guns each required a six-horse team to draw them and were organised in batteries of six guns. The 3.3 inch shell could be fired a distance of 7,000 yards and each gun was capable of firing eight rounds a minute. [IWM Q4065]

John Edward Bull and his brother George were two such young men. Their father was a baker in Daventry Street before the war and family members also owned a Market Hill grocery shop on the corner of Chickabiddy Lane. The brothers enlisted on the same September day in 1914 at Valcartier in Ontario. Their sister Ada who had gone out to Canada with them enrolled as an Army Nurse. John and his brother served in the same (4th Central Ontario) Battalion of the Canadian Infantry. On April 10th 1916 John Bull was killed in action near Dickebush on the Western Front within a few hours of his Battalion commencing their tour of duty in the front line trenches at 'The Bluff'. He was 21 years of age.

The Courier reported that the Rev. Ronald Beresford Irwin, Southam's indomitable Chaplain, had been wounded in Mesopotamia [Iraq]. It also reported that he had been awarded the Military Cross for 'Gallantry and distinguished service in the field'. He had been posted to Mesopotamia from service in France where he had been twice mentioned in despatches and had also won the Military Cross! It was a rare distinction to have been awarded this decoration twice in two widely-separated theatres of war.

As already announced by the Government, conscription for married men was introduced in May. There were exemptions for those who were deemed to be employed in jobs essential to the war effort. Tribunals were set up to hear appeals from employers who wished to dispute the call-up of men in their employ.

At Whitsun, the Government decreed that all clocks were to be advanced by one hour. The 'new' time would be known as British Summer Time. This was to be a purely temporary arrangement for the duration of the war! In the trenches on the Western Front a new item of personal equipment made its appearance. A steel helmet to give protection against shrapnel was issued to troops, to be for ever known as a 'tin hat'.

Britain was shocked to learn of the death of Lord Kitchener the popular Secretary for War. Kitchener was travelling to Russia for a conference on board the cruiser *Hampshire* when she was sunk with the loss of all hands after striking a mine off the Orkneys.

Another former Southam man was killed in action on June 3rd serving with the Canadian Infantry. Ernie Owen was one of the sons of Ernest Clinch Owen the landlord of the Dun Cow Inn in Daventry Street. In civvy street he was employed in one of the large flour mills in Ontario. He had enlisted twelve months earlier at Kenora and was serving as a Lance Corporal with the 52nd (New Ontario) Battalion Canadian Infantry.

In late May 1916, the Battalion were just coming out of the front line after an eight-day tour of duty during which they were subjected to constant heavy shelling. Their CO expressed his concern in the unit War Diary about the state of his men's health – 'Men becoming in critical condition owing to the prolonged periods under constant and heavy shell fire and relief very much needed, 8 day tours under these conditions very much too trying, 6 days would be ample'.

The Battalion came out of the trenches at the end of their 8-day ordeal with the men 'very tired and spent'. They paraded to Poperinghe for the men to have a bath but later the same day information came that the enemy had exploded two mines and had captured trenches close to Sanctuary Wood. Just before midnight, Company Commanders were briefed and given orders for a counter-attack by the Battalion at dawn on June 3rd.

The operation, like so many others during the war was hamstrung through failures of communication and poor intelligence. A bright, clear dawn began to break before the Battalion had arrived in position for the counter-attack. Men were caught out in the open in broad daylight and came under machine gun and rifle fire and an intense artillery barrage. The signal for the attack to commence did not appear at dawn and no guides had been furnished to help locate the position from which the attack was to be launched. The War Diary recorded that the country was unknown to the officers and men. Many of the Company Officers were killed and the Battalion Colonel, Lieut.Col. Hay was reported 'disappeared' believed blown to pieces by a high explosive shell. Many of the men spent the day of June 3rd out in the open taking what little shelter was afforded by shell holes, with no orders, and little idea about what was going on. It was a disastrous action for the Canadians who under other circumstances would not have been in the line on that bright Summer morning.

In the Summer of 1916 the British opened their first major offensive against the Germans on the Western Front. The plan was for the BEF to capture the German front line defences from Montauban to Serre in the rolling chalk downland of the river Somme in Picardy. For the first time, men of Kitchener's New Army Divisions were to be exposed to the rigours of a major infantry action. Half a million troops were assembled for the 'big push' which would smash through the German lines and allow the cavalry divisions to be deployed to break the stalemate in the trenches. Prior to the attack, a week-long bombardment of the enemy lines had been taking place to destroy the German trenches and to cut gaps in the huge fields of barbed wire which protected their front lines.

These 8 inch howitzers seen in action at The Battle of the Somme in August 1916 formed part of the British Heavy Artillery. Capable of firing a 200lb shell almost six miles such guns would have been used to bombard enemy positions prior to an offensive. The consequences of men in front line trenches being struck by such projectiles are unimaginable. [IWM Q5817]

On the morning of the attack on Saturday July 1st, British gunners fired a quarter of a million shells in a barrage that was heard on Hampstead Heath in north London. A number of huge mines were exploded under the German trenches and at precisely 7.30am the British infantry fixed bayonets and scrambled somewhat clumsily out of their trenches. They were laden down with full packs and various items of equipment weighing almost 70 pounds. As the British Divisions tramped slowly towards the German lines, a terrible truth was soon manifest. Contrary to all expectations, the enemy defences had not been destroyed and were largely intact. As the British artillery bombardment lifted, the German defenders came up from deep shelters hauling with them their machine guns. As the waves of BEF infantry advanced across No-Man's Land they were cut down in their tens of thousands by gun fire and machine guns. By the end of that hot July day the British Army had lost over 57,000 officers and men. Nearly 20,000 men lay dead or dying out on the battlefield under a scorching sun. It was a disaster quite without parallel in British military history. As on previous occasions, it marked merely the opening phase of an offensive operation that was to fall woefully short of hopes and expectations and which would cost the British alone almost half-a-million men before it was called off four months later. Two local men died on the first day of the battle and another half dozen would be killed on the Somme before the end of November.

The Somme 1916. Machine gunners wearing anti-phosgene gas helmets man a Vickers Mk 1 water-cooled machine gun which would be operated by two men. Unlike the Germans, the British were slow to realise the battlefield potential of machine guns. At the start of the war only two were allotted to each infantry battalion. Later in the war the Machine Gun Corps numbered 159,000 other ranks alone. In an attack on High Wood in August 1916 British gunners fired more than one million rounds from ten such Vickers guns during a 12 hour period. [IWM Q3995]

Arthur Adams was a Southam born man and the son of a butcher, Henry, who lived in Banbury Road. He was resident in Reddish, Cheshire and had enlisted in Manchester into the 21st Battalion of the Manchester Regiment. This was one of the so-called Pals Battalions raised by civic dignitaries and local recruiting committees in the larger towns and cities in response to Kitchener's appeal. In Manchester alone, eight such Battalions were raised.

The 21st Manchesters were part of the 91st Brigade reserve. The Brigade was tasked with the capture of a German trench known as Danzig Alley which ran through the village of Mametz and also with the capture of Bunny Alley and Fritz Trench. The action at Mametz was one of the few British successes on July 1st. No-Man's Land here was narrow and few shells impeded progress. German machine gunners however took a heavy toll of the Manchesters, one of whose Battalions was almost completely wiped out.

North of Mametz at Gommecourt, two British Divisions were assaulting German positions in what was a diversionary attack. The 1/14th London Regiment (London Scottish) had rehearsed their part in the action a month previously. A 'dummy' layout of the position at Gommecourt had been marked out near the village of Halloy. One of those who had taken part in the dress rehearsal was Southam man Ernest Pratt. The London Division went over the top at the appointed hour of 7.30am guided by lines of tape placed out in no man's land the previous evening under the cover of darkness. The men of the London Scottish moved forward with their 4 companies side by side. The smoke screen put up to protect the advance was much thicker than during the rehearsal and men became disorientated. A heavy artillery barrage was opened on the men as they crossed the neutral ground but in spite of everything they pressed on and managed to get into the German front line trenches. The fighting in the trenches was desperate with German bombing parties making sustained counter-attacks. By 4.00pm in the afternoon the Battalion was out of small arms ammunition and had used every bomb [hand grenade] including those recovered from casualties lying out in no man's land. Although they had succeeded in taking their objective, the position was untenable and there was no alternative other than an orderly withdrawal back to the British lines. When the roll call was taken, of the 870 men who had gone into action, 600 of them were not present to answer their names. Ernest Pratt was just one of the scores of London Scottish who were posted as missing in action never to be seen again.

In the Ypres Salient the war of attrition continued unabated. William Pittom was killed on July 2nd serving with the 2nd/5th Battalion Royal

Warwickshire Regiment. The Warwicks were in trenches in the 'Moated Grange' sector near Neuve Chapelle. Both sides staged regular Trench Raids at night on each others lines to keep the enemy on their toes and to take prisoners whilst causing as much damage as possible. The Warwickshire's front line was subjected to an intense bombardment by the Germans at 9.00pm on the night of July 1st immediately prior to such a raid. The War Diary reported that the trenches for 50 yards were obliterated and serious damage was done along the whole of the line. This action probably cost William Pittom his life. He was a married man and was living in Yardley Wood in Birmingham when he enlisted.

At a little terrace house in Napton Road, Southam, quarry worker Alf Devenport had just received news that his son Alfred (junior) had been injured during the first week of fighting on the Somme. Alf and his wife Louisa had brought up seven children in the two-up, two-down cottage past the Tollgate Farm and all of their four sons had volunteered for active service.

Young Alf was serving as a Gunner with the 108th Heavy Battery of the Royal Garrison Artillery. The news of his injury elicited an immediate response from his father. Alf (senior) decided that he would set off straight away to travel to France to visit his stricken son although he had no information as to his whereabouts. On July 8th a postcard was delivered to Napton Road saying – 'Arrived at Folkestone last night and going to sail this afternoon – Alf'. There is every reason to believe that Alf made the crossing to France. It isn't known whether he succeeded in making his way to the military hospital at Etaples where his son had been taken. Louisa received news that young Alf had died of his injuries on July 7th. His personal effects were returned along with a signed photograph of his girlfriend Win, sent with her 'best love & wishes' and dated July 10th 1916, three days after he was killed in action.

Another of Alf's sons Arthur was also in the front line on the Somme with the 6th Battalion of the Leicestershire Regiment. The 6th Battalion was one of four Leicester New Army Battalions that made up the 110th Infantry Brigade. The Battalion had been in reserve and was not committed during the opening phase of the campaign. On July 14th it was tasked for a dawn attack to assault German positions on a ridge that ran from Longueval to Bazentin le Petit. The attack was launched at twenty minutes past three on the morning of the 14th and events took a now familiar course. Many men were killed by an artillery barrage and heavy machine gun fire as they crossed No-Man's Land. When they gained the German trenches they came under enfilade fire and repeated counter-attacks by bombers throwing hand grenades. The Leicesters held and consolidated their positions and

Private Bill Abbott, 2nd Bn.
South Staffordshire Regiment.

L/Cpl Ernest Clinch Owen,
52nd Canadian Infantry.

Private Alfred Devenport, 108th Heavy
Battery, Royal Garrison Artillery.

Private Arthur Devenport, 6th Bn.
Leicestershire Regiment.

were relieved by the King's Own Yorkshire Light Infantry on July 17th. Over half the Battalion (some 500 men) were reported killed, wounded or missing. Arthur Devenport was one of those killed in the action. Alf Devenport arrived home to be given the news that two of his soldier sons had perished within a few days of each other in the 'big push.'

At Trones Wood, the 6th Battalion of the Northamptonshire Regiment and the 12th Middlesex were engaged in an action to clear the Germans out of heavily defended positions in the wood. Led by Colonel Maxwell of the Middlesex Regiment, companies of both Battalions advanced through the wood spread out in line abreast with fixed bayonets as if on a pheasant shoot. Some commentators considered this one of the finest actions of the War. During the attack Sergeant Boulter of the 6th Northants won the Victoria Cross, the first member of his Regiment to gain the award. Among those in the ranks of the Northants was Fred Constable,

Printed specially for this work]   *[By E. A. Holloway.*
SERGEANT W. E. BOULTER GALLANTLY ATTACKS SINGLEHANDED
A MACHINE-GUN TEAM.

Following an attack on German positions in Trones Wood on July 14th 1916 Sergeant William Boulter of the 6th Bn. Northamptonshire Regiment was awarded the Victoria Cross. Southam man Fred Constable also serving in this battalion was killed in the action. The illustration was commissioned for the book Deeds that Thrill the Empire.

a Southam man. Fred had had a rather unpromising start in life having been born an illegitimate child in the Southam Union Workhouse. His short and undocumented life came to an end amid the shattered trees and rotting corpses in a French wood on Saint Swithin's day, July 14th 1916.

High Wood, known locally as the Bois des Fourcaux stands on a ridge on the road between Martinpuich and Longueval. In the Summer of 1916 it was behind the German Second Line and was heavily fortified. Attempts to take the wood during the early phases of the Battle of the Somme were entirely without success.

On the afternoon of July 20th, the 2nd Battalion Royal Welsh Fusiliers were ordered up to High Wood to support a faltering attack which had been in progress since first light. As the Battalion moved up, an eye witness recalled how hordes of rats came across their lines, 'They made a noise like wind through corn. It was uncanny'. The RWF had only just come out of the front line and as they waited in Flat Iron Valley under a road bank many men were killed by enemy shell fire. The Fusiliers entered the wood and through sheer determination and courage had over-run the entire wood within an hour. The Battalion's CO Lt. Colonel Crawshay observed 'I have never seen such magnificent and wonderful disregard for death as I saw that day'. Some of the Battalion's 'old hands' who had fought at Mons said it was worse than anything they had faced before. Casualties in the 2nd RWF came to 11 officers and 238 rank and file. One of those killed was Henry Hodges a Southam-born man who had lived latterly in Stockton. Another Southam man, Private John Duckett, was one of those who distinguished themselves in the action being awarded the Military Medal. Also engaged in the attack was a young Captain in the 2nd RWF who would achieve great distinction after the war as a poet and novelist. Robert Graves subsequently wrote about the taking of High Wood in his best-selling biography *Goodbye to All That*, one of the classic memoirs of the war.

High Wood was not held after the attack by the Welsh Fusiliers on July 20th. The British were forced to withdraw and it was two months before the wood finally fell to the allies. It was not possible to clear the wood after the Armistice. It is said that the wood is the final resting place for some 8,000 British and German dead.

In late August, several Battalions of the Royal Warwickshire Regiment were in trenches near Ovillers la Boiselle which had been captured some weeks before. The 1/8th Royal Warwicks were bivouacked near the village of Aveluy where the trenches were reported to be in a truly dreadful state. The Warwicks were providing as many men as possible for working parties in Skyline Trench. The trench was full of discarded German equipment, filth and bodies. The trench sides were blown in and the whole area was a patchwork of huge shell holes filled with the corpses from the previous fighting. The men labouring in the trenches were under constant artillery fire from German positions. Ernest Arthur Pratt was wounded at Aveluy on August 27th and was subsequently reported missing. He was a local man who had enlisted in Southam.

The Government announced that the approaching August Bank Holiday was to be cancelled as also was Bonfire Night. White bread was banned due to an acute shortage of wheat flour. Dr Walter Lattey having worked tirelessly in Southam for a host of causes in support of men away at the war decided that his professional skills ought to be employed on the field of battle. He had been granted a commission in the Royal Army Medical Corps and left to take up his military duties.

Away from the mud and squalor of the Western Front, the Allies were engaged in 'sideshows' in many other parts of the world. Over a quarter of a million men were deployed in neutral Greece. In September, the Allies launched a major offensive in the mountainous terrain between northern Greece and Serbia where the Bulgarians and Germans were dug in. Henry Morby from Banbury Road in Southam was serving in Greece with the 2nd Battalion of the Gloucestershire Regiment. The Glosters were in the village of Bala where the Battalion had spent several days working on their defences. Their diarist records the problems caused by strong winds and dust which were a great hindrance to the men's work. On the evening of Sunday October 1st, the enemy launched a strong attack on the Gloster's trenches which continued throughout the night. The attackers were driven back by rifle fire and artillery barrage but responded with heavy shelling from a field artillery battery. The Battalion lost 53 men killed and wounded in the defensive action at Bala. Henry Morby was one of those mortally wounded. He died of wounds on October 2nd and is buried in the Military Cemetery at Struma. He had married a Southam girl Annie Gaskins in 1900 and the couple baptised eight children at Southam. Their last child Rose was christened just six weeks before her father's death in Greece.

The traditional Guy Fawkes bonfires were not built in Southam in 1916. On the Somme, the battle dragged on into the late Autumn before the deteriorating weather brought to a premature end a campaign marked by monumental loss of life and negligible gains. Three more Southam men were to die on the Somme before the official date of the end of the battle on November 18th.

William Gould was killed by shell fire serving with the 2nd Bn. Rifle Brigade on Sunday November 12th. Originally from Hognaston in Derbyshire he had married the daughter of Henry Glenn the Southam whitesmith. Before the war he had worked for the Southam Cooperative Society.

On the following day William Abbott was killed in action with the 2nd Bn. South Staffordshire Regiment at Serre. Bill Abbott came from an old Southam family who were well known in the district as agricultural contractors. His parents lived in Coventry Road and his brother Dick was also serving on the Western Front.

Within a few days another Southam man was reported killed on the Somme. William Smith was a Private with the 4th Bn. Grenadier Guards. His Battalion was in trenches near Guedecourt when they came under heavy artillery fire and sniping.

As the end of the year approached, there was little optimism about an early end to the war. Neither side had achieved any of the breakthroughs that had been hoped for at the start of the year. Both the Allies and the Germans had sustained enormous losses on the Somme and at Verdun. The third Christmas of the war was the bleakest yet and on the Western Front the cold Winter rains once again turned the battle field into a quagmire.

The Government appointed a Food Controller to regulate the consumption of foodstuffs and to take control of all vacant land for food production. In a piece of pre-Christmas political chicanery, Herbert Asquith was replaced as Prime Minister by David Lloyd George. Many people within the coalition Government felt that the war should be prosecuted in a more vigorous manner than that pursued by the ageing Asquith. The appointment of Lloyd George brought the promise of a more robust approach in the new year.

Chapter Four –

INTO THE BOTTOMLESS MUD

The fledgling year of 1917 would turn out to be the most exacting twelve months of the war not least for the civilian populations of the principal combatant nations. In Britain, the depredations of the merchant fleet by German submarines increased dramatically in the early months of the year. There were shortages of all imported goods and a scarcity of fuel. The situation was much the same in Germany where the Winter of 1916-17 came to be known as the 'turnip winter'. These shortages of basic foodstuffs and coal coincided with exceptionally severe weather and the coldest Winter in Europe for many years.

Men of 47th Divisional Artillery watering their horses in Flesquieres during the Battle of Cambrai in 1917. More transport was drawn by horses than by the internal combustion engine in the Great War. Almost half a million animals were killed or died in service with British forces. [IWM Q6316]

On the Western Front, when the temperature in London fell to freezing, there were fifteen degrees of frost in Arras. Hot tea froze in a matter of minutes and tins of bully beef [corned beef] froze into solid blocks which could only be broken up with the aid of a bayonet. Such hot meals as could be provided in the front line trenches froze to the men's mess tins before they could finish eating. Allen Harrison wrote to his brother to say that he and his colleagues in the Royal Fusiliers were in billets and were having to sleep with their boots on each night when they went to bed. 'We have to sleep with our boots in the blankets otherwise it would be an hour to thaw them in the morning. Even the bread it is necessary to keep under the blankets or else it becomes so hard by breakfast time that it is impossible to cut it'. Men later spoke about the long Winter nights spent in the front line when the light suddenly faded in the late afternoon and dawn was some sixteen hours away. Night invariably brought with it a great feeling of unease, and as the long night hours dragged by, men looked forward to the first warming rays of the sunrise and a chance to stamp their feet on the frozen mud.

In early February, William Amos was killed serving with the 1/6th Bn. Royal Warwickshire Regiment on the Somme. On February 4th the Warwicks were in trenches at Biaches and opposed by the 1st Prussian Guards. The diarist recorded the events of February 4th.

> *Heavily bombarded between 12 (noon) and 5.40pm with three slight lulls – intense bombardment 5.40 – carnage on Front, Support and Stettin lines and Communication Trenches. Raiding parties entered left of centre company (B. Co.) at 6.15pm – other parties on right and left stopped by L G [Lewis Gun] and rifle fire – S O S signals sent up at 6.15 and H Q communicated with Brigade on telephone just as lines were out – centre and left companies moved up supports – found enemy already driven out at 6.25pm.*

Bill Amos was one of 120 Royal Warwicks reported killed, missing or wounded in what must have been a fairly desperate action to repel the Prussian Guard in the fading light of a freezing Sunday afternoon. He was a local lad who before the war had lived with his widowed mother Sarah at Mill Cottages on the Welsh Road.

At Southam Magistrate's Court John Potter a Harbury baker was fined 7s 6d for being in charge of a horse and trap without a red rear light. There was evidently some sympathy for the defendant on the part of the Police. It is clear that Potter's trap was not displaying any lights at all when he was stopped by PC Baxter the local bobby. When the case came before the bench Supt. Clarke said 'Defendant might have been summoned for not having two white lights on the front of the trap, but there was a great difficulty in getting lamps at the present time'. At the same court, Thomas Wilson who gave his address as the 'common lodging house' in Wood Street was remanded to Winson Green prison on a charge of being dressed in His Majesty's uniform as a soldier without lawful authority. The accused man pleaded not guilty to the charge and said that he had never been in the Army and had bought the uniform from a deserter at Reading for 8s and had fully expected to get into trouble for wearing it.

It was reported that the Revd Ronald Irwin was invested with the Distinguished Service Order and the Military Cross (with bar) by His Majesty the King on Wednesday February 28th. *The Courier* reported that the Southam Chaplain had been congratulated by the King on the honours that he had gained and of his having been three times mentioned in Despatches. He was reported to be fully recovered from his wounds and returning to France the following week.

At the end of March, news came of the death of another of Southam's Royal Navy men. Herbert Randall had joined the Royal Navy as a teenager and had been in the service for 18 years when he lost his life on March 12th 1917. At the time of his death he was a Leading Seaman in the Submarine Service based at Portsmouth. He was one of 28 ratings who with 3 officers made up the crew of H M Submarine *E49*. *E49* was part of the 10th Submarine Flotilla tasked with patrolling the North Sea. The Flotilla H Q was aboard *HMS Lucia* on the Tees.

Conditions on board the early submarines were spartan in the extreme. The boats were squalid and smelly and stank of foul air. Only the Captain had a regular bunk and there were no washing facilities and the crudest of sanitary arrangements. The 'E' class submarines of which there were 56 in service bore the brunt of the war in the Royal Navy. They had a maximum speed of 10 knots on the surface but only 3 knots submerged when their range was reduced to a mere 99 miles. Until the introduction of wireless telegraphy the previous year, submariners had had to rely on Semaphore flags, pigeon post and the Aldis Lamp as methods of exchanging information from ashore.

On March 10th, *E49* under the command of Lt. B. A. Beal was on patrol off the Shetland Isles in company with submarine *G13*. There was a bitterly cold easterly gale blowing and frequent snow showers. The boat was being badly knocked about in the storm and Lt Beal decided to seek shelter in Balta Sound to wait for the storm to abate and to enable repairs to be made to the Wireless Telegraphy masts. *E49* arrived at Balta Sound

Divers from the Shetland Sub Aqua Club inspect the conning tower of
H M Submarine E49 in August 1988. The wreck of the submarine in which
Herbert Randall lost his life lies in Balta Sound in 110 feet of water.
[Royal Navy Submarine Museum 12,233]

on the following day and the repairs were successfully completed. On leaving the Sound next day to resume patrol the submarine struck a mine at the harbour entrance laid by the German submarine *U 76* two days earlier. The bows of the boat were blown off and she sank in 16 fathoms of water with the loss of all hands. Herbert Randall was the eldest son of the landlord of the Bowling Green Inn in Coventry Street. He had been born and brought up in Southam and at the time of his death was married and living in Portsmouth. He was probably one of the longest-serving men on the boat. One of those who perished was Henry Arm a Boy Telegraphist who was just sixteen years of age.

Great excitement was caused in Southam when at 2.30pm on the afternoon of Thursday March 29th a serious fire destroyed three thatched cottages close to the Bowling Green. The fire was said to have been caused by sparks from a neighbouring chimney fire. The Southam Fire Brigade were unable to control the fire because of a strong wind but the furniture of all three occupants Messrs Saunders, Shearsby and A. J. Chambers was saved.

John Duckett who had served with the Royal Welsh Fusiliers and gained the Military Medal at High Wood had been discharged from the Army as a result of injuries sustained in action. Just before Easter he got married at Southam to Annie Wood who had been one of his nurses whilst he was in a military hospital.

On the battlefields of the Western Front, the British opened a new offensive on April 9th when the Battle of Arras was launched. A few days earlier there had been a significant development when the United States of America declared war on Germany. The Battle of Arras commenced in blowing sleet at 5.30am on the morning of Easter Monday. The Canadian Corps were to capture the hitherto impregnable German positions on the high ground of Vimy Ridge and for the first time in the war all of the four Canadian Divisions would attack together. The preparations for the attack were meticulous and comprehensive. The Canadians had raided the German lines on a regular basis to gather intelligence and the attack had been repeatedly rehearsed in the weeks leading up to it.

Another of Southam's 'ex patriates' was serving in the ranks of the 10th (Alberta) Battalion of the Canadian Expeditionary Force. Leonard Bertie (Bert) Carter had emigrated from the family home on Tattle Bank before the war and had lied about his age when he enlisted. Like so many young men keen to see action at the war, he 'put back' his date of birth by twelve months when the Attestation Papers were filled in at the recruiting office in Walkerton, Ontario on January 13th 1915. In the week prior to the Vimy action, the 10th Battalion had spent many days rehearsing the attack behind the lines at a Training Ground at Estree Cauchie. Continuing bad weather and a heavy fall of snow on April 5th had hampered the Battalion's preparations.

The Canadian action at Vimy Ridge was an unqualified success. By nightfall, all save a small area of the ridge had been captured through the combined efforts of 100,000 men of the Canadian Corps. Success on the Western Front was however always achieved at a price and 3,600 men were killed on that Easter Monday. Bert Carter was one of those killed in action. He had been in France for only seven months and was twenty years of age.

Another young Southam man was also killed in action during the Battle of Arras within a few days of Bert Carter's death. Edward Hincks's family had farmed at Broadwell before the war and moved to Holt Farm, Southam on the Welsh Road in 1912. As a schoolboy Edward Hincks had attended Lawrence Sheriff school in Rugby. An accomplished horseman, the young Hincks lied about his age when he enlisted in Rugby in the

Dick Abbott, 5th Dragoon Guards.

Private William Amos 1st/6th Royal Warwickshire Regiment.

W. C. (Tom) Collier the Southam Registrar & Relieving Officer, served with the 16th Bn. Royal Warwickshire Regiment.

Edward Hincks, 11th Bn. Middlesex Regiment.

first weeks of the war. He was barely seventeen years old and not long out of school when he joined up. Having served with the Warwickshire Yeomanry and The Lancers, Edward Hincks had been promoted to Lance Corporal and was serving with the 11th Battalion of the Middlesex Regiment when he was killed in action near Monchy-le-Preux on April 12th. A number of his platoon were killed by shell fire as the Battalion was moving up to the front line to relieve the 35th Infantry Brigade.

The ever-increasing numbers of casualties on the Western Front had led since the early months of the war to a huge expansion of the medical facilities. This increased provision also extended to the nursing and after-care services available back home in Britain. Many of the more commodious private houses up and down the land were taken over for use as temporary hospitals. These VAD Hospitals were staffed by local members of the Voluntary Aid Detachments all of whom had received formal training from the British Red Cross and the St John Ambulance Association. By the Spring of 1917 there were 24 such VAD hospitals in Warwickshire alone providing almost 800 beds. By the end of the war the total number of extra beds in Warwickshire would be double that number.

The Southam & District VAD Hospital opened on April 7th 1917 after what the Red Cross described as 'many trying and unfortunate difficulties' which were not disclosed. The hospital occupied The Springs, a large

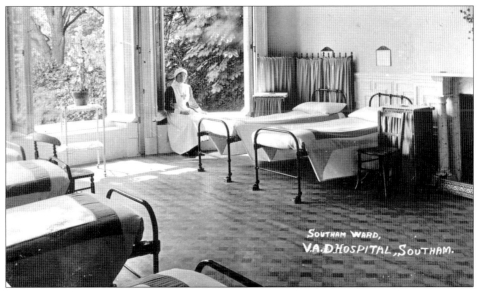

A ward at the Southam VAD Hospital opened at The Springs in Coventry Road in April 1917. The hospital had 53 beds and received cases from military hospitals.

detached house in Coventry Road which had at one time been owned by Captain H. F. Leicester Locock. The Springs [later known as The Grange] was the largest private house in the town and Locock was president of a number of local sports clubs whose team photographs were frequently taken on the steps in the garden there. The Southam hospital had 53 beds and received cot cases referred from military hospitals where men's injuries had earlier been assessed. Lady Shuckburgh was appointed Commandant. Dr Ormerod a Southam GP undertook the whole of the medical and surgical work at the hospital giving his services free until the War Office insisted on paying all medical officers in auxiliary hospitals. *The Courier* reported that Mrs Ackroyd was the Assistant Commandant and Miss Irwin and Mrs Lousada from Stoneythorpe Hall were Quartermasters. Other members of the resident staff included Sister Clipstone and Nurses Hillier, Tolley, Green and Sykes.

Harry Flowers was killed in action on April 28th near Arras during a pre-dawn assault on German lines. One of three Southam brothers serving in the Army, Harry was a Private with the 5th Battalion of the Royal Berkshire Regiment. Following the attack which was not successful, two dozen members of the Battalion were never seen again and were posted 'missing in action'. Harry Flowers was one of them.

The British made plans for another attack on the same German trenches which Harry Flowers and his colleagues had unsuccessfully assaulted a few days earlier. Spearheading the attack was the 8th Battalion Royal Fusiliers. The second attack was called off when some of the gas released into the enemy trenches prior to the assault drifted back among the Fusiliers. The Germans immediately opened a tremendous artillery barrage on their attackers. Private Allen Harrison a local man was among those killed. He was a relative of Alf Martin the saddler whose shop was in the High Street. His Adjutant Captain Royle wrote to Alf Martin to inform him that Allen who was a Signaller had been killed on May 1st while on sentry duty in the front line near Arras. His typewritten letter added 'The cause of his death was a shell of heavy calibre which burst quite close to where he was standing and I myself was only about 6 yards from him. His death was instantaneous and he did not even groan or say a word so he could not possibly have felt in any way, any pain whatever'.

David Gillmore died of wounds in trenches near Fresnoy on the Arras Front on May 12th. He had enlisted at Southam and was serving with the 16th Battalion Royal Warwicks. The Battalion's front line had been under a concentrated artillery bombardment for several days which led inevitably to many men being killed or seriously wounded. Young David Gillmore was only nineteen years old, his parents lived in Leamington Road near to the Lilley Smith memorial.

The Rev. John Hart-Davies, Rector of Southam died on Sunday May 27th at the age of 78 after a long illness. He had exchanged the living of St James's, Bristol with the former Rector of Southam Revd E. F. Neep in 1895 and had been Rector for twenty two years. Two of his sons who were both pilots with the Royal Flying Corps were granted leave to attend the funeral conducted by the Archdeacon of Coventry.

In mid-June, the Headmaster of the Boys' School Mr Grassam left to join His Majesty's Forces and was presented with an air pillow and some cigarettes by his former pupils. The Royal Family thought it prudent to dispense with their Germanic titles of Saxe-Coburg-Gotha and instead to adopt the rather more English surname of Windsor.

Tom Masters, a Staff Sergeant with the 236th Brigade Royal Field Artillery was killed in action on June 2nd at Barlin. His father John had for many years run an ironmongers shop in Coventry Street. Tom was in business in Folkestone at the outbreak of hostilities and was married with two children. He had been in the Territorials before the war and went out to France in the early months of the war.

Local newspapers reported that private Frank King of the Royal Warwickshire Regiment who had previously been reported missing in action had been wounded and was a Prisoner of War in Turkey. His mother had heard nothing of him for six months. Second Lieutenant Bernard Lee son of the former Southam Police Inspector was reported to have suffered gunshot wounds in the face serving with a Royal Field Artillery battery in France. Sergeant Sam Griffin of the Royal Engineers, son of William Griffin of Coventry Street was awarded the Meritorious Service Medal. Sam had been 15 years in the Army and had spent 9 years soldiering in China and Gibraltar. By the end of June over 10 million men had volunteered for Military Service in the USA and the first of them were just setting foot on French soil.

On the first anniversary of the Battle of the Somme, two more Southam names were added to the roll of the fallen. Horace Parkinson the son of Samuel Parkinson the manager of the High Street branch of Lloyd's Bank died of wounds received in action. Horace Parkinson was another Old Laurentian and was serving with the 1/4th Leicestershire Regiment as a subaltern. He was seriously wounded whilst leading his platoon in a large-scale raid on German trenches at Lievin on June 6th and was evacuated back to England where he died in a military hospital on July 1st. He was buried in Clifton Road Cemetery in Rugby.

Lance Corporal William Bleloch was also killed in action on July 1st 1917. His family farmed at Fox Farm, Bascote Heath and before the war he had worked as an Engineering Draughtsman. He had joined the Queen's Own Oxfordshire Hussars, a Yeomanry Regiment, in 1910 and had been in France since the outbreak of hostilities having been badly wounded in an action at Zouave Wood in the Spring of 1915. In July 1917 the Hussars were at Guillemont Farm which occupied an important and isolated point in no man's land between the German and Allied trenches. William Bleloch and his squadron were asleep in a dugout having been relieved at 3.00am in the morning when at midday a chance German shell landed on their position instantly killing Bleloch and three other Hussars. The Hussar's historian described William Bleloch as 'a man of iron nerve; no danger ever ruffled him; a good brain and a clear head, quick to grasp essentials.' One of his officers wrote to his parents to say that William had seen a lot of severe fighting and that his squadron had been encouraged by the example he had set. He was buried in the British Cemetery at Templeux-le-Guerard.

Stan Baldwin of Napton Road was reported wounded and in hospital in France suffering from shell shock. He had been twice gassed during his twelve months on the Western Front. The war was said to be costing £7 million pounds a day. Ronald Irwin the Army Chaplain narrowly escaped death when a shell burst a few yards from him wounding him in the thigh.

The town was stunned to hear that Lieutenant Ivan Hart-Davies the elder son of the late Rector had been killed in a flying accident on the eve of his departure to join a fighter squadron in France. Ivan Hart-Davies had qualified as a pilot with the Grahame-White School at Hendon before the war. At the time of the fatal accident he was piloting a Bristol F2b fighter aircraft (A7103) from the aerodrome at Northolt in Middlesex. The coroner's inquest heard evidence that when at low altitude and about to land, the aircraft suddenly nose dived into the ground from 200 feet. Hart-Davies was killed instantly, his observer Lieutenant Miller a Rugby man was seriously injured but survived the crash.

Ivan Hart-Davies was described by the obituary writers in the local newspapers as a 'man of many parts' and it can be truly said that this is something of an understatement. As a schoolboy at the King's School, Canterbury he played cricket, football and hockey for the school and also won competitions for athletics, cross-country running and swimming. In adult life he played cricket for Warwickshire, rugby football with Moseley and hockey for Rugby. He won bob-sleigh races in Switzerland although

Ivan Hart-Davies, Royal Flying Corps.
A photograph taken after his graduation as Flying Officer in August 1916.

he had never taken part in the sport before and he enjoyed mountaineering, golf and a host of outdoor sports and games. He had held a number of endurance records for both motorcycle and light car. In 1913 he had set a new motorcycle record for the John O'Groats to Land End run when he covered the 886 miles on a three and a half horsepower Triumph in a time of 29 hours 12 minutes. Before the war he had set up in business in Rugby as an Insurance broker.

The funeral took place at Southam on Tuesday July 31st 1917 with full military honours and former members of 35 Training Squadron Royal Flying Corps acting as bearers. The remains of Ivan Hart-Davies were interred in the old part of the churchyard near the chancel door and close to where his father had been laid to rest two months earlier. He was 39 years of age.

In August the local Tribunals met to consider representations made by local employers on behalf of employees who had been conscripted. A crippled farmer from Priors Marston was granted temporary exemption from call-up for his nephew a single man aged 23 without whom he would be unable to manage the farm. The case of Frank Rainbow a 32 year old married Southam butcher was adjourned in the hope that a single man in similar employment in the district could be found and released for military duty with Frank Rainbow then taking over his duties in addition to his own. A married Stockton canal toll collector aged 38 produced a certificate from the Canal Control Committee which exempted him from military service. Mr W. P. Bourne a local solicitor and high bailiff of the Southam County Court met with less success before the Warwick Appeals Tribunal. His appeal on behalf of his son Cecil, a single man who acted as his sole assistant was dismissed.

The Courier reported that a large number of munitions workers had spent a well-earned holiday in Southam and the neighbouring villages. The 'Wounded Soldiers Hospital' was reported to be 'quite full up again' and undergoing frequent changes of patients who were said to be much enjoying the full benefits of country life. The 212 members of the Southam ('D') Company of the 2nd Battalion Warwickshire Volunteer Regiment were supplied with Lee Enfield rifles of the latest pattern and eagerly awaited the arrival of their first consignment of uniforms. The men had been waiting for their kit since the outbreak of the war three years earlier!

Two local men were killed within a few days of each other in August. Tom Worrall and John King were the same age and both had worked for Kaye and Co at the Southam cement works before joining up. They enlisted together into the Royal Artillery in October 1915 and did their training together before going out to France. John King died of wounds on August 8th serving as a gunner with the 2nd/1st (Warwick) Battery of the Royal Horse Artillery. At the time of his death, the battery was in action near Wulverghem in the Ypres Salient attached to the 3rd Australian Division. John King's parents lived in Banbury Road. His pal Tom Worrall was killed in action on August 16th with the same battery. His mother wrote to his Commanding Officer to ask about the circumstances of her son's death and on August 28th she received a handwritten letter on a page torn from a book of graph paper. The letter which was signed by 2nd Lt Stratton described how 'his subsection had just finished firing and he and the gunners were coming away from their gun when a hostile plane flew over and dropped a bomb in the midst of them. Your son died instantly and I'm sure suffered no pain'. Such words of reassurance would have brought scant comfort to his parents who had three other sons serving in the war.

Pencil written letter sent by Tom Worrall to his mother before his embarkation for the front to join the Warwickshire Horse Artillery.

A group of Royal Horse Artillery men photographed at camp in England.
Tom Worrall is ringed, second from the right in the back row.

The surviving brother of the two Hart-Davies flyers narrowly escaped death over the battlefields of the Western Front shortly after returning to duty following his brother's funeral. Hugh Hart-Davies had been commissioned into the Royal Field Artillery and held the rank of Second Lieutenant. He had been attached to the Royal Flying Corps and although not a qualified pilot, he flew as an Observer with 48 squadron commanded by W. Leefe-Robinson. At 5.45pm on the afternoon of Sunday August 19th 1917, Hart-Davies was observing for his pilot Richard Dutton in a Bristol F2b fighter (A7171) when they were engaged in combat by two enemy aircraft over Ostende. During the ensuing dog-fight the Bristol went out of control and crashed behind the German lines. Both men were posted 'missing in action' by their squadron. Many weeks later the Red Cross received information that Hugh Hart-Davies had survived the crash and although injured was alive and being held in a Prisoner of War camp in Hamburg, his pilot Richard Dutton had been killed.

It was in an aircraft such as this that both of the Hart-Davies brothers met with misfortune. The Bristol F2a known as the Brisfit first flew in 1916 and initial deliveries went to 48 squadron. Subsequently modified to become the F2b it was one of the best general purpose aircraft of the war and enjoyed a lengthy post-war career. [E (AUS) 5524]

As the war entered its fourth year there was no sign of an end to hostilities and few expectations of any Allied breakthrough. The pupils at the Girl's School were granted a half-day holiday so that they could pick blackberries to be made into jam for the soldiers and sailors serving in the war.

Another old boy of the Congregational Church Sunday School was killed on the Western Front. William Hancocks was serving with the 1st Battalion Coldstrean Guards when he was killed on September 21st. His brother Jesse had been killed earlier in the year serving with the Warwickshires in Mesopotamia. The men's parents lived at Green End in Long Itchington and when news of William's death reached his mother Nora she was greatly concerned. Two of her three sons had perished in the war and she feared for the life of her sole surviving son Fred who was serving in the Middle East with the Royal Welsh Fusiliers. Nora wrote to the War Office in London to ask whether in the light of the sacrifices already made by the family if her son Fred could be released from the Army. His CO was contacted in Alexandria and Fred was called in and told that he would be released but he would have to make his own way back to England. It took Fred many weeks to get home. He walked for 150 miles across the Arabian Desert following the camel trains to Port Said where he managed to hitch a lift on a steamer going to Limerick in Ireland. His feet were badly blistered as a result of his long trek through the scorching desert sand and he carried the scars of that experience till his death many years after the war had ended.

On the Western Front, the Allies had launched another major offensive in the Ypres Salient to seize the high ground running from Staden to Gheluvelt and then to drive north to the Dutch frontier. The action would come to be known as the Third Battle of Ypres but was for ever after called by the name of one of the tiny villages set as objectives. The village was Passchendael and the campaign was one of the most appalling in the annals of warfare.

The new Allied offensive in the Ypres Salient was dogged with bad luck from the outset. It had been planned to use massed tanks to break through the German defences and by so doing to make a large-scale artillery bombardment unnecessary. Such bombardments churned up the marshy ground over which the infantry had to advance and made their task much more difficult. As it was, insufficient numbers of tanks were available and a bombardment became a necessity. The offensive had been delayed by several months and when it at last began it coincided with the wettest August for over seventy years.

The continuous shelling by 2,200 artillery pieces and the incessant rains turned the whole battle area into a huge swamp. The ground over which the Allies were to advance became a featureless morass of water-filled shell holes. There were no recognisable features of any description. Villages, farms and woods had all been reduced to low mounds of pulverised nothingness. In the months since the Battle of the Somme, the Germans had had a fundamental rethink about the way they defended their front line positions. Rows of massively reinforced concrete bunkers had been built just behind the line in which the defenders would safely shelter from any artillery barrage. After the barrage had been lifted, the attacking infantry would be raked with machine gun fire from these concrete pill-boxes.

Before the war Chateau Wood echoed to the sound of bird song. After several months of unrelenting artillery fire the area has been reduced to a featureless morass. An Australian soldier collects the identification papers from a fallen colleague.
[IWM E (AUS) 4599]

The conditions under which men fought at Third Ypres were undoubtedly the most wretched encountered during the whole of the war. Engineers had to lay down timber roadways across the huge expanse of mud so that men and supplies could get anywhere near to the front line. These 'corduroy tracks' were quickly targeted by the Germans and regularly shelled. Getting rations and ammunition to men in forward positions became extremely difficult. Horses and pack mules were widely used to transport items to the front but they often sank up to their bellies in the mud and couldn't be got out. If men or transport were forced off the plank roads, there was every chance that they would sink without trace in the glutinous pools of liquid slime. Moving up field artillery pieces to support the infantry was immensely difficult and when guns were in place they frequently sank into the mud.

Stretcher bearers carry a wounded man through mud up to their knees after the Battle of Pilckem Ridge in August 1917. The area is completely devoid of any distinguishing features. [IWM Q 5935]

A Royal Artillery officer saw a six-horse team and its wagon load of ammunition sink without trace in a matter of minutes without an opportunity even to cut the harness. Hundreds of men drowned in the stinking water-filled shell holes unable to break free from the dreadful suction. On their way up to the front line, the men of the 15th Battalion Royal Warwicks found a man bogged down in the mud which was above his knees. Four men attempted to pull him free by passing rifles under his armpits but their efforts were to no avail. Reluctantly they fell in again to resume their slog up to the front line. When the Battalion came out of the line two days later they passed by the same spot. The hapless Tommy was still trapped in the shell hole but only his head was visible and he was totally deranged. There were bodies and pieces of bodies everywhere and the numbing Autumn rain was unremitting. The mud was all-pervading. It choked rifles and machine guns and rendered them useless and it seeped into men's boots and plastered their clothing. It got into their rations and their mess tins and it was all around them to swallow them up if they put a foot in the wrong place. These were the conditions into which the 16th Battalion of the Royal Warwickshire Regiment ventured forth to attack the German stronghold at Polderhoek Chateau at twenty minutes past five on the morning of October 9th.

In happier times Polderhoek Chateau had been a rather imposing Italianate house on the Menin Road at Gheluvelt. The house had been in German occupation since the start of the war but by the Summer of 1917 British artillery had reduced it to a pile of rubble. The extensive cellars of the house had been reinforced with concrete and were seemingly impregnable. In what had been the grounds of the chateau were numbers of concrete pill-boxes many of which were linked by tunnels to the heavily defended cellars. All previous attempts to take Polderhoek had been repulsed with the attackers suffering heavy casualties.

The portents did not bode well for the lads of the Warwicks when the Battalion assembled for the attack just after three o'clock in the morning to await the start of their creeping artillery barrage. The previous day their CO Lt. Col. Deakin had expressed his concerns in the Battalion War Diary:

> *While in support the men were in a deplorable condition, the trenches were 6 inches deep in water, it rained heavily soaking everybody, and it was impossible to get them any hot food ....*

Within a few hours this hungry, shivering and dispirited body of men were to be hurled against a host of German machine gunners concealed in underground bunkers behind several feet of reinforced concrete. The outcome of the action was entirely predictable and the events of the day are recorded in the unit diary for October 9th 1917:

> *5.14am. Our barrage commenced and appeared to be short, this was afterwards confirmed by "B" company who were scattered by it.*

> *7.00am. I proceed to the front line to find out the position and discovered that the Battalion were back in the line from which it jumped off. It appears that there had been heavy casualties ... from MG's [machine guns] firing from pillboxes.... In view of the heavy casualties and state of the men and the constant MG fire I decided that it was not possible to reorganise and make another attempt later on, and gave orders to my officers to reorganise and remain where they were.*

Owing to the shortness of time to prepare the attack, it had been impossible to explain thoroughly to all the men how far they were to go etc. Consequently when the casualties occurred, they did not know what to do, and returned to their jumping off trenches. Another factor in the situation was the condition of the men. They had been five days without any hot food, soaked to the skin by the heavy rain that fell, and owing to the state of the ground and the constant heavy shelling, very little rest or sleep had been possible for them.

10.25am. Message from OC 'B' Company to say enemy reported massing on left flank. I informed Brigade to the effect.

11.30am. Message from 15th Inf Bde to say dig in and hold on.

12.10pm. Message from 15th Inf Bde to say 2 companies of 15/Royal Warwicks will dribble up in small parties for the purpose of repelling counter attacks – they will relieve part of the front tonight.

From 3.50pm to 6.10pm enemy heavily barraged Battalion HQ and pill-boxes in line with it.

The relief for the hard-pressed Battalion did not reach them for a further 24 hours. They came out of the line at 12.45am on the morning of October 11th. The following entry was made in the diary:

STRENGTH 'over the top'	*20 officers*	*514 other ranks*
CASUALTIES during operation October 5 – October 10th 1917	*13 officers*	*291 other ranks*

In less than a week, the Battalion had lost over half of its men in what came to be known as the Battle of Poelcapelle. Among the Battalion's dead was William Collier. William Collier known locally as Tom, was a Rugby man by birth who lived in Warwick Road Southam. He was well known in the town having been Relieving Officer for the Southam Rural District for 13 years before joining up in the Autumn of 1916. His first wife Mabel had died in 1911 at the age of 37. He had married again the following year and was survived by his second wife Gladys and an eleven year old son named Frank born to his first wife Mabel in 1906. He was thirty eight years of age.

Also killed on the same day was Arthur Duckett. He was serving with the 11th Battalion of the Royal Warwickshire Regiment who were part of 112th Infantry Brigade (37th Division). His Battalion was in support in the Tower Hamlets sector when he was killed by shell fire. The Battalion had found great difficulty with their transport and with the carrying of rations 'on account of intense darkness, damage of tracks and heavy shelling'. Arthur Duckett was the youngest son of John and Julia Duckett and had worked as a baker in Leamington before enlisting.

On what under normal circumstances would have been Southam Mop Day came news of another local man's death. Harry Baldwin from Warwick Street was mortally wounded by artillery fire whilst serving with the 2nd/1st (Warwick) Battery Royal Horse Artillery. Harry was a driver with his battery and was the third Southam man to be killed with the battery within a few weeks. He was a married man aged 27 when he died of wounds in the Advanced Dressing Station at Duhallow on Monday October 15th.

On October 26th a renewed offensive was launched in the sector which came to be known as the Second Battle of Passchendael. Private Edward Turner was serving with the 1st Royal West Kent Regiment part of 13 Brigade (5th Division) along with two Battalions of the Royal Warwicks. The RWK's were to attack down the valley of the Scherriabeek river. The two Warwickshire Battalions on the left and centre were to attack Polderhoek Chateau. The Royal West Kents found it impossible to make any progress along the valley which was an impassable marshland. The Warwicks managed to clear the chateau and the park but by nightfall the British attack had been repulsed and the attackers had been forced to fall back to their original line. The Germans reoccupied the chateau. Edward Turner was posted 'missing in action'. He was the third of six children born to his parents and one of four brothers serving in the forces.

On the day that Edward Turner was reported missing, another Southam man Private George Sturley of the King's Own Royal Lancaster Regiment was being commended by his CO for gallant conduct and devotion to duty in the field near Poelcapelle. It was also announced that Corporal John Fell, Royal Field Artillery, one of the men who had gone out to France on the first day of the war had been awarded the Military Medal for bringing in wounded men under heavy fire. *The Courier* also reported that 27 members of the local Volunteer Corps under 2nd Lt Plummer had been called out for patrol duties one evening in response to a Zeppelin alarm in the town. The regular meeting of the Southam Board of Guardians was also reported in the newspaper. The Master of the Workhouse Mr Charles

Shirley reported that there were currently 44 inmates in the Workhouse, a reduction of ten on the previous year. An advertisement for an Assistant Nurse had produced just one applicant who later withdrew when she secured a position nearer to where she lived.

Private George Sturley's Commendation for Gallant Conduct and
Devotion to Duty in the field at Poelcapelle.

The Battle of Passchendael was called off on November 10th. Haig's armies had advanced their front lines by about four miles at the cost of some 62,000 dead and 164,000 men wounded. The losses on the German side were even greater. In Russia there was a second revolution when the Bolsheviks staged a bloodless coup. News filtered through of plans by the Workers' and Peasants' government to begin demobilisation. If the Bolsheviks entered into a separate peace treaty with the Germans, it would enable the transfer of almost a million German troops and huge numbers of field guns to the Western Front. Such a prospect occasioned considerable misgivings in the minds of the Allies.

The new Rector of Southam was presented by His Majesty The King, the Crown being the patron of the living. The 'new man' at the Rectory was the Rev. Osborne Mills Jones BA one time Assistant Master of Cleethorpes Grammar School and more recently Vicar of Ferry Hinksey, Oxford. The living at Southam was considered to be better than most and O. M. Jones found his stipend almost doubled as a result of his translation up the Coventry road. His appointment was something of an inspired choice and the likeable and enthusiastic little Welshman stayed for over thirty years and became a well-loved figure in the town.

Revd. Osborne Mills Jones BA was appointed Rector of Southam in October 1917 following the death of John Hart-Davies.

Arthur Hughes (on the left of the group) lost a leg in the war and was invalided home in late 1917.

In early December Fred Baldwin was killed in action. Fred had been serving as a Gunner with the artillery since the outbreak of the war and had seen action in many of the major engagements in the Ypres Salient over the previous three years. He had been both wounded and gassed and was with 157 Brigade RFA when he was killed at Lapin Farm on December 4th. Although well behind the lines, the gunners came under daily fire from German artillery and many men were killed and wounded each month. Numbers of men were gassed by enemy shells. Frederick Baldwin's parents William and Elizabeth lived in Leamington Road, Southam. He was a married man aged 26. His wife Ethel lived at 243 West End Lane in West Hampstead, London.

As in previous years a local committee organised Christmas presents for all the Southam men away at the war and 241 individual parcels were sent out at an average cost of six shillings each. It was discovered that six men had somehow been overlooked and as soon as the error came to light a whist drive and a dance were speedily organised to provide the necessary funds for parcels for the unlucky six.

Just after Christmas there was news of the deaths of two more Southam men, both on December 28th. Joseph Fennell was a Private with the Royal Army Medical Corps in Italy when he contracted pneumonia and died. He had been born in Southam and as a boy lived in Coventry Street. He had married his wife Annie at Southam before moving to Bordesley Green in Birmingham. At the time of his death he was serving with 70th Field Ambulance in a field hospital at Trevignano near Padua. He is buried in the main cemetery in Padua.

Henry Glenn was nineteen years of age when he died of wounds on the Somme. His father Henry was a Southam whitesmith whose family lived in a small terraced house next to the Red Lion in Coventry Street. The circumstances of young Henry's death are not known. His Battalion (2/7th Royal Warwicks) were not in the line when he died. At the start of December the Battalion was in a very depleted condition and could muster barely a hundred men. The nominal strength of a Battalion would normally be almost ten times that number. In the week before Christmas the Battalion had been in support and had been quartered in tents. The weather had been particularly inclement with periods of fog, rain, frost and snow and a strong north-easterly wind. On Christmas Eve they took up residence in some barns at Sailly Laurette. There were no beds and little comfort for the men who settled down to sleep on the bare earth floor. Henry Glenn is reported to have died of wounds on Friday December 28th.

On the last day of the old year, Southam readers of *The Daily Mail* were surprised to see in its columns a photograph of two local brothers. Sergeant W. H. Poulton and his brother Private Walter Poulton who had both been awarded the Military Medal within a few days of each other. Walter was reported to have been discharged from the Army after being three times wounded in action. Before his discharge he managed to gain a bar to his MM.

As 1917 came to an end there was no prospect of peace. Throughout Europe people were suffering the torments of a war that had dragged on for four years. Hunger and starvation stalked the streets of many once prosperous cities. In Germany more than a quarter of a million civilians

BROTHERS WIN THE M.M.—Sergeant W. H. Poulton, Staffordshire R., and Private W. Poulton, Royal Warwicks, who won the M.M. within a few days of each other. The latter, who was three times wounded, has now received his discharge.

Photographs of the two Poulton brothers were published in The Daily Mail on December 31st 1917.

had died of hunger during the year. 1917 had proved to be a year of unremitting adversity for all those in the Ypres Salient. The abiding memory of all who had served there over the previous twelve months was of the stench of death and the ubiquitous mud. Siegfried Sassoon wrote:

I died in hell
(They called it Passchendael) my wound was slight
And I was hobbling back; and then a shell
Burst slick upon the duckboards; so I fell
Into the bottomless mud, and lost the light.

Chapter Five –

TO THE LAST MAN

Epiphany Sunday 1918 had been appointed by the King as a Day of Prayer and Thanksgiving and was observed at Southam with special services. At the parish church the morning choral communion was attended by the Volunteers, the Scouts and the Soldiers and Nurses from the VAD hospital. The Rector read the King's Proclamation from the pulpit which exhorted his people 'to pray that we may have the clear-sightedness and strength necessary to the victory of our cause.' The Roll of Honour of those who had given their lives, which hung in the church for names to be added was read out.

One of the new Rector's first priorities had been to resuscitate the *Southam Parish Magazine* which had been defunct for many years due in part to the poor health of John Hart-Davies in the latter part of his incumbency. The first edition of the re-published *Southam Parish Magazine* appeared in January 1918 and bore news of Southam men serving in the war. Private George Shorthouse one of the Warwickshire Yeomanry to have survived the sinking of *The Wayfarer* in 1915 was reported to be a prisoner of war in Germany.

In London the Government decreed that, because of a grave shortage of food and particularly of meat, restaurants would not be allowed to serve meat on two days of each week. The regulations would not apply where a full meal cost 1s 6d or less. For the first time, many eating establishments were able to tempt the palates of their more discerning diners with a hitherto unknown delicacy – vegetable sausages. The VAD hospital at The Springs continued to be the focus for much of the entertainment put on in the town. The Seven Sparks Pierrot Troupe put on a concert for the wounded soldiers as did the pupils of the Infants' School who were granted a half-day holiday to perform for the patients.

The remains of another young Southam man were brought back home for burial on February 6th. Sidney Hughes was another teenager destined to have his life cut short by war. He was nineteen when he died in hospital at Edgbaston on February 3rd. He had served as a Driver with the Royal Army Service Corps and had been brought up in Appendix [Pendicke] Street in the little cottage adjoining the Primitive Methodist Chapel. Before enlisting he had been a member of the Scouts and had sung in the Parish Church Choir. His former choir colleagues sang at the funeral held with full military honours with members of the Volunteers acting as bearers.

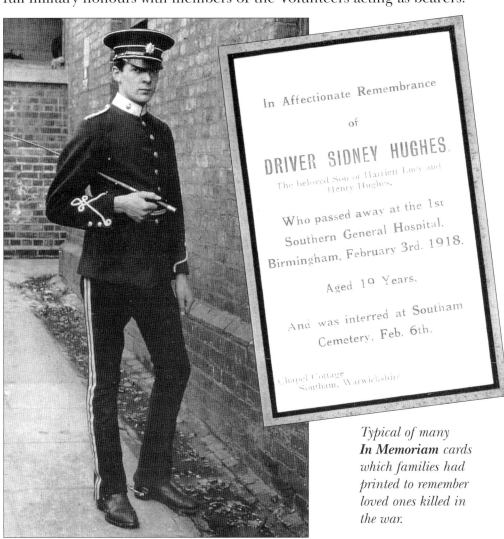

In Affectionate Remembrance

of

DRIVER SIDNEY HUGHES,

The beloved Son of Harriett Lucy and Henry Hughes,

Who passed away at the 1st Southern General Hospital, Birmingham, February 3rd. 1918,

Aged 19 Years,

And was interred at Southam Cemetery, Feb. 6th.

Chapel Cottage Southam, Warwickshire

Typical of many **In Memoriam** *cards which families had printed to remember loved ones killed in the war.*

Sidney Hughes served as a driver with the Royal Army Service Corps and died aged 19 in the Southern General Hospital, Birmingham on February 3rd 1918.

The following week, the second of the three Flowers brothers from Appendix Street was killed in action. Percy Preston Flowers had left school and gone to work as a grocery assistant for Thomas Bull on Market Hill staying on there when the business was taken over by George Adams. He joined up in October 1916 and served with the 1/6th Bn West Yorkshire Regiment.

In February 1918 the Battalion was at Devonshire Camp near Reninghelst in Divisional reserve and providing men for working parties repairing trenches at Westhoek Ridge. Each day 9 officers and 320 other ranks paraded before at 5.00am for their work details. To get to the trenches took three hours and involved travel by bus and train and then a route march to their respective work stations. The men worked for four hours under the supervision of Royal Engineers before falling in at noon for the return journey to camp, arriving back at 3.00pm. Percy Flowers was one of three men killed on February 12th whilst with the working party. The unit diary also records on the same page that 'the sentence on Pte W. Gibson had been promulgated'. A few days earlier Gibson had been tried by general court martial for desertion at Etaples and had been sentenced to death by firing squad. During the war over 3,000 such death sentences were passed by military courts. The majority of sentences were subsequently commuted as was that passed on the unfortunate Private Gibson but over three hundred men were executed mainly for desertion and cowardice. Gibson was sentenced to 10 years penal servitude.

By March, the Allies' fears about the capitulation of the Russians were fully realised when the new Bolshevik regime signed a peace treaty with the Central Powers in the process ceding huge tracts of land. With the Eastern Front inactive, the Germans were in a position to launch a major offensive against the Allies before the arrival of significant numbers of troops from the United States.

At home the consequences of the war became ever more serious. Meat, margarine and butter were all put on ration which was also extended to coal and other fuels, all of which were in desperately short supply. The Headmaster of the Boys' School received two printed leaflets from the Ministry of Food entitled *Delicious Stews* and *Thirty four Ways of Serving Potatoes*. The publishers of *The Courier* announced that the price of the paper would be increased to 2d due to the continued scarcity of newsprint the production of which had fallen to just a sixth of pre-war levels.

In France and Flanders the Spring would usher in a critical phase for all those at the sharp end of the war. The Allies did not have long to wait for the threatened German offensive. At 4.40am on the morning of March

A group of staff and patients on the lawn of the Southam VAD Hospital.
Patients in VAD hospitals wore a standard blue tunic and trousers
with a red tie but were allowed to wear their regimental caps.

21st a tremendous artillery barrage was opened up on the Allied lines.
When it was lifted five hours later waves of German Infantry appeared out
of the thick early morning fog and fell on the British in the Forward
Zone. In many places the British front fell apart. As the day wore on there
were huge losses and the situation quickly deteriorated as the 5th Army
began to fall back in retreat.

Captain Eric Lattey was with the 3rd Battalion of the Worcestershire
Regiment in the Arras sector near Louveral where the Germans had
broken through the British lines previously held by the 51st (Highland)
Division. Arrangements had been made for a counter-attack involving
74th and 57th Infantry Brigades but in the event the plan could not be
implemented and the Worcesters received orders to withdraw just as a
determined German infantry attack was launched on their lines. Eric
Lattey's company were pinned down in their hastily dug trenches
bordering a sunken road. There was no way they could withdraw without
being cut down. There was no alternative but to engage the Germans.
During the course of Friday March 22nd Eric Lattey found himself in
charge of 'B' company. He was the third Company Commander the men
had had that day. Both Captain Lett and 2nd Lt Hemus had been killed
whilst leading the company. The Worcesters came out of the line three
days later and so did Captain Lattey.

Captain Eric Lattey (MC and bar) photographed after the war at his wedding to Mary Brewster in Southam on June 19th 1926. He was Captain of Southam Cricket Club whose members formed a guard of honour near the south door of the parish church. Fred King is one of those holding bats aloft.

Ernest Hollis another Southam man was among those reported missing in the Worcester's action at Louveral. His parents must have hoped against hope that news would soon come of his internment in a German POW camp or that he was perhaps in a Military Hospital somewhere in France. They waited in vain for any news of Ernie and as the months passed nothing was heard of him. Their son had gone off to war as a fresh-faced lad of 19 and nothing was ever seen or heard of him again. After the war his name was carved on the Arras Memorial to the Missing. It is one among 35,942 names of men whose families had harboured similar hopes for the return of much loved sons, fathers and brothers whose lives had just been obliterated in the blinking of an eye.

Lieutenant Bernard Lee was also killed in action on March 22nd serving with 'D' battery of the Royal Field Artillery. The battery was in a quarry at Ste Emilie when the enemy bombardment commenced and they came under a rain of gas and high explosive shells. The German artillery fired many millions of rounds of mustard gas, phosgene and diphenylchlorarsine over the first two weeks of the campaign. Within a short time some of the front line trenches were overrun. The RFA men had a frantic time trying to hook up the gun-teams to get their 18 pounders safely away. Throughout the 21st and 22nd of March the battery managed to execute an ordered withdrawl from the position at the same time maintaining a sporadic fire in response to SOS signals sent up front the British lines. Bernard Lee was one of sixty members of the battery to be killed during two days of turbulent activity. He was seriously wounded on March 21st and died of his wounds the following day. His fellow subaltern 2nd Lt Woodland was also killed, he had only been posted to the unit the day before. Bernard Lee's father had been Inspector of Police at Southam for several years before being promoted Superintendent and moving to Stratford-on-Avon in 1911. Bernard was 23 years old and had enlisted in the RFA as a Gunner in 1914 being commissioned the next year. Prior to the war he had been assistant chemist at Southam Cement Works and was also a keen athlete, choirman and bell ringer at the Parish Church.

Saving the Guns.

A postcard by E. W. Savory Ltd depicts Artillery men saving their 18 pounder guns in the face of enemy shelling. It was in just such an action that Lt. Bernard Lee was killed.

In the latter months of the war, many soldiers were seriously incapacitated by exposure to mustard gas contained in artillery shells. Mustard gas had been developed to harass rather than to kill unlike the earlier toxic gases. Exposure to just one part of the gas in ten million parts of air would lead to massive blisters, severe headaches, a rise in temperature and pulse and pneumonia. In greater concentrations men's lungs were burnt out and their eyes and faces completely eaten away by the gas. Their bodies were covered in first-degree burns. The gas was practically odourless and no counter-measures were ever discovered to combat its terrible effects.

Private Alf Fennell was one of those gassed during the German Spring Offensive in 1918. Alfred had served with the Royal Warwickshire Regiment prior to being attached to the Labour Corps. It is quite probable that he had been wounded or gassed previously which would account for his transfer to a non-combatant unit such as the Labour Corps. He was gassed at the front and died in hospital at Devonport on Easter Saturday. He was brought back to Southam and buried with full military honours a week later on Saturday April 6th.

The situation on the Western front continued to deteriorate for the Allies as they struggled to defend successive lines. On April 11th Haig issued a Special Order of the Day which concluded 'There is no course open to us but to fight it out. Every position must be held to the last man: There must be no retirement. With our backs to the wall and believing in the justice of our cause, each one of us must fight to the end'. No one better understood that than Captain Lattey and the men of the hard-pressed Worcestershire Regiment. The 3rd and 4th Battalions had been in continuous action for almost three weeks. The Regimental historian recorded their state of readiness.

> *All were so utterly tired that it was impossible to remain awake. Neither officers nor men had slept for more than half-an-hour consecutively since the battle began. In the clear light of a Spring morning they dug, or fell asleep over their spades and could not be awakened. Men talked thickly and without meaning, drunk with weariness. But by infinite labour the trenches were dug deep enough to provide cover by the time the German guns found the line.*

After dark that same day the Germans broke through the centre of the line of the 3rd Battalion and seized the summit of a small hill the Mont de Lille. From there they were able to open fire on the Worcesters from behind the Allied lines. The over strained troops gave way and for a few minutes there was danger of a general panic. Captain Eric Lattey rallied the young soldiers and with a subaltern organised a counter-attack on the German positions. The small group stormed the hill and killed or captured all of the enemy party. Thirty prisoners of 2nd Jagers and 1st Bavarian Jagers were captured and three light machine guns taken. For his action that day Eric Lattey was awarded the Military Cross.

On the day that Eric Lattey was winning his MC young Arthur Rathbone was blown up by an exploding high explosive shell fired in all probability from a British gun. In common with his contemporaries, Arthur had left school at the age of 13 and had gone to work for Mrs Chamberlayne at Stoneythorpe Hall. When war broke out he was just 17 and not old enough to enlist. His employer had been most insistent that he should do something for his country and her unrelenting lobbying bore fruit when he signed on at the Coventry Ordnance Factory for munitions work. On his eighteenth birthday he enlisted and went out to France with the 1st Battalion of the Royal Warwickshire Regiment.

Private Arthur Rathbone, 1st Battalion Royal Warwickshire Regiment.

On April 15th orders had been issued for the Warwicks to attack and capture Pacault Wood and some fortified enemy buildings on the outskirts of the wood. The British artillery barrage fell short and behind the advancing companies of the Warwicks. In a few minutes the barrage came down on the Battalion's headquarters and two companies who were waiting to cross the Canal d'Aire on a pontoon. In the course of the day many of the Warwicks were killed by their own artillery and machine gun fire. The Battalion lost 225 men in the abortive attack on Pacault Wood. Arthur was just one of them. He was 20 years of age.

Arthur Rathbone had previously been wounded and invalided home suffering from trench feet and the effects of gas. He had spent many weeks at home lying flat on his stomach gasping for breath. The shortage of manpower was such that he was subsequently passed fit for duty and returned to his unit in France.

As Arthur lay struggling to get his breath in the front room of the family cottage on Abbey Green, through the window his sister Hilda watched the comings and goings of the butchers boys on their overburdened delivery bikes. As she sat with Arthur and ministered to his needs she became aware of something that to her seemed somewhat strange. The front window of the cottage faced onto Warwick Road where lived some of the town's more well-heeled residents. She didn't understand why on any number of occasions she had seen Grant's delivery boy passing the window with his front basket fairly laden with things wrapped in greaseproof paper. Whenever she and her mother had gone into Grant's the butchers, where they had been regular customers for many years, there was never anything other than a few bones on offer 'to make a nice soup' and never any 'proper' meat.

What Hilda had noticed had not gone unnoticed by others in the town. In May 1918 Mr John Oldham, gentleman, and his wife Selina of Beech Hurst, Warwick Road appeared before the Southam magistrates accused of food hoarding. John Oldham was a church warden and among his other duties was Chairman of the local Food Committee of which his wife was also a member. When the case came before the Bench, evidence was laid that when a food inspector accompanied by Inspector Scott of Southam Police searched the defendant's premises ten hams were found in calico bags together with two sides of bacon and 'a quantity of other provisions'. One of those who gave evidence of having supplied two hams and two sides of bacon was Ethel Grant the daughter of Mr T. G. Grant, butcher.

In a rare appearance by barristers in the Southam courtroom it was argued on behalf of the Oldhams that five of the hams had been purchased for friends and the other five were never intended for their own consumption. The bench thought that the purchase of such quantities of food for a household consisting of two adults and two servants was quite in excess of their requirements. At the conclusion of the proceedings the charges against John Oldham were dismissed. His wife was found guilty on three charges and fined 10 shillings on each charge with costs of £8. 4s. It was perhaps a salutary lesson to all those who were minded to use their social standing in the community to get round the laws which most other folk had to observe. The soldiers at the VAD Hospital were the unwitting recipients of several hams from an unnamed local benefactor.

After the debacle in Gallipoli, the Warwickshire Yeomanry had spent much of the war fighting against the Turks in the sands of Sinai and Palestine. At Huj they had taken part in what turned out to be the last Cavalry charge by the British Army. After the surrender of the Turks the Regiment re-formed at Belah and in March 1918 their CO Colonel Gray Cheape announced that they had been selected for dis-mounted service as machine gunners in France and were to leave for the Western Front, news that was received with mixed feelings.

A group of Warwickshire Yeomanry Troopers encamped in the sands of Egypt prior to their departure for the Western Front and the sinking of the Leasowe Castle.

The Regiment was *en route* for the first leg of the journey to Italy and had embarked on May 26th on *HMT Leasowe Castle*. At 12.25am the next day the *Leasowe Castle* was struck by a torpedo on the starboard side. The men's previous experience of being torpedoed evidently served them well on the second occasion. Under a full moon and on a calm sea, most of the Yeomanry were rescued. The Southam men were among those who again survived a sinking. Unfortunately, over a hundred men were lost including eleven members of the Warwickshire Yeomanry. The Officer Commanding, Lt Col Gray Cheape was one of those drowned.

In Southam news came that Private George Adams had been badly gassed and was in hospital in London with damage to his eyes. His brother had been killed in 1916. 2nd Lt. J. F. Stratton was also reported to have been gassed and a patient in a French hospital. Frank Bleloch, the brother of William was serving with the Lancashire Fusiliers and had been taken as a prisoner of war during the German Spring Offensive.

At The Springs there were problems with obtaining a supply of water for the hospital. There was no mains water in Southam which relied solely on wells and boreholes. It fell to the lot of some of the patients to make a number of trips each day to Tomwell Pump in Welsh Road to fetch water for the hospital. The former supply had been condemned. Thanks to the skill of the Bishops Itchingon 'dowser' Mr T. Garrett a good supply of water was located at a depth of 16 feet in the orchard. Miss Irwin continued her regular trips down to London to bring back medical supplies for the hospital invariably travelling in Rawbone's model 'T' Ford to Rugby station to catch her train.

In Mountfield Gardens, the three young Griffin boys had noticed that the hutch which had hitherto housed their pet rabbits was suddenly and somewhat unexpectedly empty. Their worst suspicions were confirmed the next day when they sat down for dinner. Unless they were very much mistaken, what was served up was rabbit stew!

The continuing shortages of manpower and the hugely increased burden of administering the food rationing regulations necessitated the help of several teachers from local schools. The Boys' School was closed on a number of occasions so that teachers could assist with the work of the local food office. The headmaster wrote in the school log book 'It appears that the Director [of Education] expects that I shall be required to join the army shortly and therefore arrangements have been made for Mr Walton of Bishops Itchington to take charge in the event of my going'.

The Courier reported that General Sir Francis Treherne KCB, DSO, had visited the VAD Hospital with the County Director of the British Red Cross.

'7.8.'17.

Dear Mrs Worrall,

It is with very deep regret that I have to write to inform you of the death of your son, No. 614603 Bombardier T. Worrall. He was killed while doing his duty in action yesterday.

Your son was such a good fellow & we all feel his loss very much & do most sincerely sympathise with you. Apart from being a good soldier, his good influence in the Battery was very great.

The O.C. wished me to write to you as he is still with the guns & unable to, himself at present

I feel sure it must be some comfort to you to know he died doing his duty.

Believe me,

Yours sincerely,
C.G. Stratton,
2/Lt
2/1 Warwick R.H.A

This letter written by a subaltern on a page carefully cut from a book of graph paper is typical of many tens of thousands of similar letters sent to next of kin informing them of the death in action of a loved one. Written by 2/Lt Stratton to Tom Worrall's mother in August 1917.

The General had addressed the patients and expressed his satisfaction at the running of the hospital. The paper also reported that the Rev Ronald Irwin had again been mentioned in despatches and after a short furlough would be taking up a new appointment as Assistant Chaplain General at 4th Army Headquarters. Jack Powell from Stockton learned that he had been classed Grade 1 for active service having been turned down on no less that sixteen previous occasions. The spiritual needs of workers in the Coventry munitions factories were of concern to clergy members of the Southam Rural Deanery. At a garden meeting at Beech Hurst it was reported that large hostels had been built in Coventry to house several thousand girls and young women employed in the local factories. The young women had been recruited from places as far afield as the Channel Isles and Russia and there was general concern as to their moral and spiritual welfare.

Private Frank Hancox died of wounds on June 5th serving with the 10th Battalion Royal Warwickshire Regiment. He had been seriously wounded in the leg on the previous day as a result of an exploding shell and had had the injured limb amputated. He had lived opposite The Crown in Daventry Street where his father Joe was a carpenter and local chimney sweep.

Men of the Royal Army Medical Corps loading wounded on to an ambulance train near Doullens in April 1918 following the German Spring Offensive. All of the stretcher cases have been taken directly from the battlefield and are in full service dress complete with boots. Six out of every ten men who served in the war became casualties. [IWM Q8752]

A group of Tommies pose rather self-consciously round a harmonium. The hymn singing is accompanied by a ukelele with saucepan lid percussion and is conducted by a Dispatch Rider. Immediately behind the organist is Southam man Fred Plummer, (Warwickshire Yeomanry)

Harry Bicknell died of wounds in a German hospital on the following day. He had been previously wounded and hospitalised in England before being taken prisoner during the German Spring offensive. The circumstances in which Harry Bicknell met his death are not clear. The *Southam Parish Magazine* reported that he had died in a German hospital on June 6th of wounds in the left upper thigh caused by shell fragments dropped from an airship. By the Summer of 1918 the deployment of airships over the Western Front had long since ceased. Their use was by that date confined to naval protection and maritime reconnaissance. It seems more likely that the camp in which Harry Bicknell was interned in occupied Belgium was damaged in an Allied air raid by bombs dropped from conventional fixed wing aircraft. The use by both sides of aircraft for bombing strategic targets had increased dramatically. On June 2nd the Germans claimed to have shot down 38 allied aircraft for the loss of

17 of their own. Harry Bicknell was well known in Southam having been a member of the Fire Brigade. He had also been Captain of the Southam Rugby Football XV and a keen cricketer. Before the war he had lived in School Street and had worked as an Insurance Agent.

Thomas Rockingham was killed in action with the 15th Bn Royal Warwickshire Regiment on June 30th. Towards the end of June the time was thought to be ripe for a British offensive. The Royal Warwicks as part of the 5th Division were to play a major part in 'Operation Borderland' near the Nieppe Forest. The Battalion had rehearsed the attack in the preceding days and everything went according to plan with little opposition. 'The defenders were bayonetted or otherwise dealt with and a few prisoners sent back to Battalion HQ' to quote from the rather prosaic entry in the War Diary. Twenty six other ranks were killed in the action and another six died of their wounds over the following days. Tom Rockingham's death was recorded on June 30th. Two of his brothers-in-law (the Flowers brothers) had already been killed in action. Thomas was the second son of George Rockingham of Daventry Street a retired Metropolitan Police Officer. Before the war he was a painter in the employ of Greaves, Bull and Lakin at their Stockton cement works. *The Courier* reported that his three brothers were all serving with the forces.

By midsummer of 1918 there were a million American troops in France and their supplies were being unloaded on French docksides at the rate of 20,000 tons a day. The arrival of the Americans on the Western Front was to have a significant and decisive impact on the war. Quite unexpectedly there appeared on the battlefield a new and extremely potent source of mortality. It came not in the form of weaponry or noxious gas but as a virus that had been around to plague mankind for generations. An outbreak of influenza, so-called Spanish 'flu started in June in India and Britain spreading in a few months to become a world-wide pandemic. It would wreak havoc around the world. On the Western Front it would kill more American soldiers than would enemy bullets.

On August 8th the Allies opened a major offensive along the Western Front when the Battle of Amiens was launched. The Canadian Corps moved into position near Amiens under a shroud of secrecy and launched their attack on August 8th. The Germans were driven back 12 kilometres on the first day of the offensive. The 4th Canadian Infantry Battalion was one of those units taking part in the attack. One of those killed was Sergeant George Riley Bull an expatriate Southam man whose only brother John had been killed in action in April 1916. George Bull had been awarded the Military Medal in July 1917.

A week later Private William Harold Seckington died of wounds at La Clytte following an enemy artillery bombardment. He was serving with the 11th Bn Queens Royal Regiment when he died on August 13th. Three days earlier the Queens had absorbed the 2nd Bn 107th Regiment from the United States of America. The Battalion was reorganised into 2 composite Battalions 'A' and 'B' each made up of 2 British and 2 American companies. William Seckington lived and enlisted at Southam having been born at Helmdon just up the Welsh Road in Northamptonshire.

Another Southam man was killed before the month was out. Edward Shearsby had been christened Edmund Thomas when he was baptised at Southam in 1891. His parents lived in a little close of cottages that faced the Red Lion across Coventry Street. As a young man Edward had gone to Badminton House in Gloucestershire to work for the Duke of Beaufort in the kennels of the Beaufort Hunt. He had served in France for three years and was killed with the 12th Bn Gloucestershire Regiment at Irles on August 25th. The Gloucesters had been engaged in several days of heavy fighting along the Arras – Albert railway line and had lost over 300 men.

The fighting now took on a much less static appearance and the widespread use of tanks by the Allies began to have an impact. The war entered a mobile and decisive phase.

The Courier reported that Sergeant W. H. Usher whose mother lived in Daventry Street had been taken as a prisoner of war and was being held in Germany. His brother Harry was serving in Egypt with the Royal Garrison Artillery. Also in the local news was Nurse M. I. Tolley from Vivian House on Market Hill who had received a commendation from the War Office for her valuable services at the VAD Hospital.

It was also announced that the Rev R. J. B. Irwin, Assistant Chaplain-General to the Fourth Army in France holder of the Distinguished Service Order and the Military Cross had been awarded the Croix de Guerre by the French Authorities. The citation set out in detail how on 18th May 1918, when an attack by hostile aircraft caused an explosion at an ammunition dump in a built-up area he immediately made his way there to see what help could be given. He had worked for several hours with absolute disregard for his own safety to ensure that all those civilians whose lives and properties were endangered by the explosion got away safely.

In his biography *Forty Years a Soldier* written after the war, Irwin's former Divisional Commander, Major General Sir George Younghusband described him as 'one of the bravest fellows in the Division ...... a small man and lame from birth but with the heart of a lion'. He went on to add

The Rev. Ronald Irwin DSO, MC, Croix de Guerre. After the war he became Vicar of Lillington before being appointed Archdeacon of Dorking. He died in 1930 aged 49 from wounds received in the war.

'I should have given him the Victoria Cross myself but there are all sorts of rules and regulations which, perhaps rightly, hedge this decoration about. Anyway, Padre Irwin earned the Victoria Cross half a dozen times".

He describes an incident when after an unsuccessful attack on Turkish positions, hundreds of British wounded lay out in the open in pouring rain many within a few yards of the enemy trenches. Padre Irwin spent the hours of darkness taking food and water to the injured Tommies and comforting those mortally wounded, at the same time and even though unarmed, driving off bands of marauding Arabs who appeared after every battle to loot the dead and dying.

Throughout August the Allies continued to push back the Germans on the Western Front. By the end of the month the Germans were preparing to evacuate Flanders and to give up all the ground they had gained in the Spring offensive. The freshness and zeal of the huge numbers of American troops now in action were to become decisive factors during the final months of fighting. In early September Field Marshall Haig travelled back to London to ask the War Office for mounted men and for equipment designed to increase the mobility of his troops in readiness for the fluid type of war that he anticipated in the 'near future'.

Arthur Baldwin was killed in action near Laventie on Friday September 13th. He was twenty years of age and had served with the Hampshire Regiment before joining the Royal Berkshires.

Eric Lattey was again in the thick of the fighting with the Worcestershire Regiment near Neuve Chapelle. The Regimental History records that by that date the company commanders were experienced in war. Eric Lattey led his company in a successful bomb and bayonet attack on German trenches in front of the old distillery at La Tourelle and for his actions that day was awarded a bar to his Military Cross.

Some miles away a young Southam lad of 19, William Garratt lay dead behind his machine gun. He was killed in action near Hooge and laid to rest in Hooge Crater Cemetery where lie two other Southam men he would have known well. William had joined up on his 18th birthday and had gone out to France the year before with the 9th Battalion of the Machine Gun Corps. His parents lived in Coventry Street where his father William was a blacksmith. Before the war he had worked as a farm labourer for Edward Cardall in Daventry Street.

By the end of the month the German Army was in full retreat along the entire Western Front. In Southam there was news of a number of local servicemen. Private P. J. (Jimmy) Ledwith who had recently joined the Royal Air Force was 'lying very ill in hospital in Dorchester.' Jimmy had been discharged from the army on account of wounds received on the battlefield and had for some time acted as a Sergeant Major in the local Volunteers. Private W. E. Boote son of the late landlord of the Black Horse was reported missing after service in India and Mesopotamia [Iraq]. The news from France at last brought some encouragement to the folk back home. After four years of suffering and adversity it was clear that the war was drawing to an end. In towns and villages throughout Britain a battle of quite a different sort was just about to begin with the arrival of Spanish 'flu.

Jimmy Ledwith and P. V. (Vic) Burnell were both on active service and were incapacitated in the war. Seen here in 1916 with a collection of pets and a piglet they were instrumental in fund-raising in the town for various causes such as the British Red Cross.

In a six-week period between the middle of October and the end of November 1918 the Southam Parish Registers record over twenty burials in the churchyard. The normal number of burials in a similar period would be two or three. On several days the Rector conducted two funerals and officiated at three on Guy Fawkes Day. Many of the victims were not elderly or those in poor health but young people who had hitherto enjoyed good health. Eleven of the local victims were under 40 years of age. Among those who died was William Langton the landlord of the Horse & Jockey and Martha Duckett whose selfless efforts in 'laying out' many of the dead resulted in her own death from the virus. Throughout Britain 150,000 Britons, soldiers and civilians fell victim to the epidemic.

On October 21st Private John Duckett who had won the Military Medal at High Wood succumbed to the 'flu aged 31. After High Wood he had been discharged from the army on account of shell shock and wounds. The *Southam Parish Magazine* described how 'though his pension was of late much reduced he would make no complaint but through frequent illness and suffering went bravely and cheerfully to work at Messrs Kaye & Co.' He was buried at Southam with full military honours on October 26th with former hospital comrades acting as a bearer party.

On November 11th 1918 the war came to a somewhat unexpected end and the fighting ceased. The sirens at the local cement works were sounded, union flags were fetched out and hung from bedroom windows and the church bells rang out in celebration. It was a Monday and the Southam womenfolk were engaged in their wash houses just as they had been on the Monday that the war commenced.

Chapter Six –

IN MEMORIAM

Although the war was over, the suffering for the participants was far from ended. There were still Southam men in Prisoner of War camps in Belgium and Germany and it would take many weeks to demobilise the hundreds of thousands of servicemen in France and Flanders. There was still fighting in the east in North Russia. An Allied Intervention Force had been sent out to Murmansk in June 1918 after the collapse of the Russian Front. Having been sent primarily to deny the resources of Russia and Siberia to the enemy, the Allies found themselves fighting a guerrilla war against the Bolsheviks.

The signing of the Armistice occasioned special services in Southam as everywhere. The Rev Ronald Irwin was back from the war and preached on the text 'Their name liveth for evermore' the words chosen for the memorials to be erected in the multitude of British cemeteries in France and Belgium. The *Parish Magazine* carried the news that in Feed the Guns Week the people in the Southam District had raised over £48,000 with the average sum per head given being £6 3s 5d. The amount raised per head by the inhabitants of Southam was a truly remarkable £16 8s 10d. Their rather less affluent neighbours in Bishops Itchington had donated 18 pence each.

There was a touch of romance at Southam VAD Hospital at The Springs where one of the convalescing patients greatly enhanced his prospects of recovery by marrying his nurse. Corporal William MacVeigh a Winchester man and Frances Gahagan were married at Our Lady and St Wulstan Roman Catholic Church in Wood Street on November 27th 1918 with Father Stanbridge conducting the ceremony. The bride received a present from the staff and patients at the hospital.

As soon as hostilities were over it was decided that the old Battalions of the army might again take over their colours which had been placed for safekeeping in the guardianship of the Church. Captain Eric Lattey led a Colour Party of the 3rd Battalion of the Worcestershire Regiment who left Fienvillers for England on Christmas Day 1918. The Party received the Colours at Worcester Cathedral the day after Boxing Day and the Battalion were able to hold a ceremonial parade with the Colours on January 18th 1919.

Lt Hugh Hart-Davies was repatriated and entered the RAF Hospital Hampstead to receive treatment for the wounds he had received when brought down in the enemy lines in August 1917. When he returned to Southam his mother was living at Whitehall in Warwick Road where she had moved after having to vacate the Rectory.

Another Southam POW came home at Christmas. George Shorthouse had survived the sinking of the *Wayfarer* with the Warwickshire Yeomanry before being taken prisoner in 1917 on the Western Front. The local correspondent of *The Courier* outlined George's experiences whilst in captivity.

> *Pte G. H. Shorthouse, Warwickshire Yeomanry, has recently returned home after 12 months captivity in Germany and Belgium. As reported in these columns at the time, he was taken prisoner on November 30th 1917 and spent the first two months at Dulmen, Westphalia, when he was moved up to the Lille front and employed loading German aeroplanes with bombs but on the commencement of our last offensive his party retired to Halle. On the signing of the Armistice, he found his way, with many others, to the British lines, tramping nearly 30 miles the last day. No rations were issued to them, and they had to depend on the hospitality of the Belgians. Pte Shorthouse can tell of the hardships suffered by our men. He himself, 13 stone when captured, got down as low as seven, but no wonder on a fare of bread and cabbage water: a loaf of bread having to serve 16 men for a day. Pte Shorthouse speaks with deep gratitude of the parcels received from the Prisoners of War Fund, without which he would have shared the fate of many of his comrades, and died of starvation. He received 40 parcels up to the end of August. Pte Shorthouse served in Gallipoli, being on the torpedoed Wayfarer, before seeing active service in France.*

The starvation diet of Allied Prisoners of War was the major cause of death of those in captivity. Because of the British Blockade of German ports many Germans were themselves starving towards the end of the war. There was too little food to go round. The diet of a POW would consist of little more than a slice of bread and what was charitably called soup but what was to all intents and purposes little more than the water in which the camp guards had boiled their vegetables. The bread was frequently adulterated with sawdust due to the shortage of flour. Men on working parties ate nettles, dandelions and even grass and for most of the time were starving. It was only the regular arrival of Red Cross parcels that kept men alive and preserved in them some hope of surviving the war.

Trooper George Shorthouse (far left) with colleagues of the Warwickshire Yeomanry in full dress uniform c.1912.

George Shorthouse was married at Southam in the Spring of 1919 but would never recover from the privations endured in Dulmen. He died on the second anniversary of the Armistice in 1920, a frail man broken in health and old before his time. He was 29 years of age.

George Shorthouse and his bride Louisa Shearsby photographed after their wedding in 1919. George was aged 27 but has the appearance of an old man – a result of his deprivations when a German Prisoner of War. He died the following year.

Arthur Turner, elder brother of Edward died in hospital at Etaples on the last day of February 1919 serving with the 2nd/7th Battalion Royal Warwickshire Regiment. Arthur had joined up in 1915 and had served in France & Italy. In the Summer of 1916 whilst on leave from the war he had married Sarah Gillmore at Southam. Both Sarah's father and her brother were serving soldiers. Arthur developed influenza just before he was due to be demobilised and subsequently died of pneumonia. He was buried in the Etaples Military Cemetery. One of his brothers and his brother-in-law David Gillmore had also died in the war.

The Allied Intervention in North Russia was coming to an end by the Autumn of 1919. The British had sent out an Expeditionary Force under General Maynard in June 1918. This force was made up of men who had previously been classed as unfit for active service. Many were classed B2 (Base duty abroad) and B3 (Sedentary duty abroad) and most had been wounded in action. The campaign had developed into a haphazard offensive against the Bolsheviks and involved troops from many of the Allied nations as well as Serbs, Finns and sundry east Europeans. I don't know how it was that a young man from Mountfield Gardens in Southam found himself in the Arctic wastes of Murmansk in the Summer of 1919. Fred Hartley had joined up at 18 and had served in France and had no doubt been demobbed after the Armistice. Perhaps it was because he couldn't find employment in post-war England that led him to sign on again that Summer. Whatever the reasons may have been, by September of 1919 Fred was a Corporal with the 19th Battalion of the Machine Gun Corps and *en route* for the Barents Sea and a landfall in Murmansk.

The terrain of Northern Russia was quite alien to men who had served on the Western Front. The country was an area of tundra, bogs and lakes with huge tracts of pine and fir forrest. The railway from Murmansk south to Petrograd provided the only means of transport in an area where there were no proper roads and only tracks which were impassable in Summer when the ice had melted.

The half Battalion of the MGC to which Frederick Hartley was attached arrived on August 27th having been sent out as a general reserve for Lord Rawlinson the C-in-C to oversee the withdraw! The Allies planned to withdraw by early October before the harbour at Murmansk became ice-bound. Maynard had a plan to clear the Shunga peninsular and the adjoining tracts of land prior to the withdrawl.

Fred Hartley was killed on September 13th in an attack on Bolshevik and Red Finn positions near the village of Kav Gora 500 miles south of Murmansk. His body was conveyed to the village of Svyatnavolok and buried in the village churchyard of the Russian Orthodox church there. The Machine Gun Corps embarked for England on October 4th on HMT *Ulua*. During the six weeks they were in Russia this half Battalion of fewer that 500 men received 3 Military Crosses, 8 Military Medals and a DCM. Their Officer Commanding, Captain W. Morris recorded the unit's actions on two sides of a sheet of paper and wrote at the top 'No Diary of Events was kept as there were no company clerks or stationery'.

The six British graves in Svyatnavolok were declared unmaintainable in the 1920's. Frederick Hartley is commemorated along with his colleagues on one of 38 individual memorial tablets set in the walls of the New British Cemetery in Murmansk. This cemetery was impossible to maintain during the Soviet era and was at one stage reported by the Soviet authorities to have been destroyed. Ten years ago and following the collapse of the Communist regime in the USSR the cemetery was discovered to still exist although badly fallen into disrepair. It is currently being reinstated and restored by the Commonwealth War Graves Commission.

The Murmansk New British Cemetery contains a special memorial to those men who died in the North Russian campaign. Fred Hartley's was one of six graves in the village churchyard at Svyatnavolok which the CWGC declared unmaintainable in the 1920's.

Joe Shearsby, Royal Artillery (note the spurs being worn).

William Henry Lake, (the author's maternal grand father) Machine Gun Corps. and the Royal Berkshire Regiment.

George Fell, Army Remount Service.

Percy Sheasby, Royal Flying Corps.

Norman Cleal, badly gassed serving with the Royal Warwickshire Regiment and photographed here when a patient in a VAD Hospital. He later served in the Royal Army Service Corps but died a young man.

Bombardier John Fell seen here with his wife Olive served with 66 Battery Royal Field Artillery and was awarded the Military Medal.

Another member of the extensive Baldwin family died almost two years after the signing of the Armistice and became the last man to have his name included on the town war memorial. Charles Isaac Baldwin had served as a Sergeant with the Royal Army Service Corps during the war and was in receipt of an army pension. He had found employment as caretaker at a Rugby school after the war and was 39 years of age when he died of heart disease at his home in Elsee Road, Rugby on August 16th 1920. His widow Sarah arranged to have his body brought back to Southam where he was interred in Southam churchyard.

In Southam as elsewhere local people were swift to recognise the sacrifices made by their fellow townsfolk who had not returned from the war. The 1919 Annual Parish Meeting appointed a committee 'to devise and suggest some schemes to a future parish meeting for a public parish memorial to our 'fallen heroes' and for the purpose also of giving a public welcome to local members of HM Forces on their demobilisation'.

Within a few weeks the War Memorial Committee had met at the Court House under the Chairmanship of Captain WC Lattey RAMC. Sub-committees were appointed to consider the various proposals which had been put forward. Three very different schemes had been proposed. The first was for the provision of a recreation ground, second was for a club and library, the third suggestion was for a memorial obelisk. In June 1919 a public meeting was convened at the Court House to consider reports from the three sub-committees.

A committee chaired by Dr Lattey reported that they had looked at two suitable sites for a recreation ground at the Park and the Bury Orchard. Since the Park formed part of the Rector's glebe there were legal difficulties attaching to its disposal. The Bury Orchard was owned by Mr Arthur Turner of Bascote House and he had agreed to sell it at the same price for which he had purchased it some years earlier which was £110 an acre. The total cost of acquiring the site and providing suitable facilities was estimated at £615.

The second committee had been asked to look at a much more ambitious scheme to provide a new building to house a club, library and slipper baths at an estimated cost of some £8,000. To provide such facilities would involve not only a large capital investment but also running costs of some magnitude. Mindful of this, the possibility of levying a local rate towards the upkeep had been canvassed with the Local Government Board. The general view of the committee was that provision of new premises was unrealistic given the cost involved. This being so, they put forward an alternative scheme for the purchase of London House [now the HSBC

Bank] on Market Hill for use as a club. The property was currently used as a drapery shop with workshops and living accommodation but the owner was prepared to sell. The total cost of purchase, alterations and furnishing was estimated at £3,500 of which £2,800 would have to be raised by voluntary subscriptions.

The third scheme suggested was the provision of a stone memorial taking the form of an obelisk to be erected on a site yet to be decided upon.

After some discussion the meeting passed a resolution that the War Memorial consist of the provision of a Public Library and Club at a cost estimated at £3,500

The local committee had also been charged with arranging suitable celebrations to mark the return of Southam's discharged soldiers. The Peace Celebration was held on Saturday July 19th 1919 but was somewhat marred by inclement weather in the afternoon.

During the morning a procession assembled on Market Hill for a parade round the town led by the Town Band and a large group of 70 discharged soldiers under the command of Captain Lattey RAMC. There were decorated floats and children in fancy dress and the Southam Fire Brigade brought up the rear. The parade returned to the church for a special service of thanksgiving at noon.

In the afternoon childrens' sports were held on a field owned by Mr John Oldham at the rear of the Abbey but many of the days events had to be curtailed due to heavy rain. The Children's Tea was given under cover in the Assembly Rooms and the day concluded with a dance there after the children had moved to the Court House where they were entertained 'to a late hour'. The planned bonfire and firework display were put off to a later date.

In August a 'Welcome Home' dinner was arranged at the Court House for discharged and serving members of HM Forces. Before the evening dinner Mr Elkington of Broadwell took group photographs of the men on the lawn of Dr Lattey's house in Wood Street. All those attending were to be given a postcard photograph to mark the occasion.

Almost twelve months after the decision had been made to proceed with the provision of a Club and Library, a further Parish Meeting was convened in May 1920 to receive reports and to consider what progress had been made.

A letter was read from Captain Lattey the chairman of the War Memorial Committee informing the meeting that his committee had failed in its objective. Of the sum of £3,500 required to purchase and

*Two views of the Southam Peace Celebrations in 1919. The group photographs of
the men who had served in the war were taken on the lawn of Dr Lattey's house in
Wood Street. He is the man at the front of the group in the uniform of a Captain
(RAMC). The man in the straw boater is W. W. (Bill) Sturley. The house was
later demolished and is now the site of a District Council car park.*

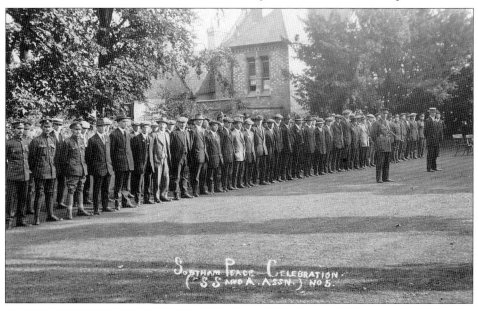

convert the London House, the committee had received in donations the sum of £253 8s 3d a mere 7% of the monies required.

Since the previous meeting Mr Arthur Turner had given the Bury Orchard to the town as a free gift for use as a public recreation ground.

'The Southam Men Who Answered Their Country's Call' march up Coventry Street headed by the Town Band and are seen passing Grants the bakers. Saturday July 19th 1919.

A view of the spectators at the children's sports held in a field behind The Abbey in Warwick Road. The starting gun carried by the man on the right appears to be a standard infantry issue Lee Enfield rifle.

Of the three options which had been originally mooted, there was now only one left for consideration. Mr W. H. Plummer proposed and Mr J. W. Spencer seconded that an obelisk be erected in memory of those who had lost their lives in the Great War, the type and position of this to be determined by a future Parish Meeting. Before the motion could be put to the meeting Captain Lattey proposed an amendment seconded by the Rector O. M. Jones that the memorial consist of a stained glass window in the Parish Church. On a show of hands the original proposition was carried by a large majority. A small committee was elected to raise the necessary funds for the erection of an obelisk.

Various fund-raising activities were organised on behalf of the War Memorial Fund which progressed satisfactorily. By late June of 1920 the sum of £198 had been raised and the position and final details of the monument were being discussed.

When the question of the siting of the memorial came before the committee in August 1920 the appointed architects Messrs F. P. Trepass & Son of Warwick were able to report on four possible sites in the town for the memorial.

1. This was a site in the corner of the Rectory garden facing Archers the chemists shop. This would involve removing part of the Rectory garden wall and a large elm tree and would involve site work costing about £100.

2. This was an area to the left of the church steps again requiring some excavation and site work which was estimated at £70.

3. The gun platform on Market Hill. This was next to the weighbridge at the lower end of Market Hill. The Parish Council had paid for the construction of a concrete platform on which it was intended to display a German artillery piece donated by the Lord Lieutenant of the County. In the event, the German gun had already been found a permanent home by some Southam men and lay partly submerged in the Sowe brook. The architects's view was that the erection of a Gothic cross on this site would appear somewhat incongruous against a backdrop of brick shop fronts of no particular design or style.

4. The favoured and most suitable site for the memorial was a flat area of asphalt in the churchyard close to the belfry door. No site preparation would be necessary and the whole of the monies could be expended on the memorial.

There was some support at the meeting for Trepass's first option since a parish meeting had earlier endorsed the proposal for the Rectory site.

When this was put to the meeting the resolution was lost on a show of hands and the original resolution relating to the site near the belfry was then put and carried unanimously.

The work of carving and erecting the memorial which was to be in the form of an octagonal cross was entrusted to Mr Thomas White the Southam monumental mason. Tommy White was a well-known figure in Southam. He came from a musical family and was bandmaster of the Southam Town band.

Tommy White the Southam stonemason poses by the newly completed war memorial prior to its dedication. New panels have been added to the memorial in recent years and the details of the men's units/numbers which were originally on the memorial below each name are now covered.

The memorial of Hornton stone was unveiled and dedicated on Saturday December 17th 1921 at 2.00pm. The Rector O. M. Jones conducted the service of dedication under the wan sun of a Winter afternoon. He was assisted by the Rev A. C. Esau, Rector of Stockton and by Mr Wright of the Congregational Church and Mr Clee representing the Primitive Methodist Chapel. The Town Band with Tom White conducting led the singing outside while an orchestral band accompanied the singing in the church. The unveiling of the memorial was performed by Admiral Cuming DSO, CBE, President of the West Midlands Area British Legion. At the conclusion of the service the *Last Post* and *Reveille* were sounded as the ringers rang a muffled peal and floral wreaths were placed around the base of the cross.

The marble memorial tablet in Southam Congregational Church, Wood Street.
Some of the names are not on the town war memorial in the churchyard.

The carved tablet in memory of Midshipman Alexander Lattey
in the south aisle of the parish church.

This carved oak memorial panel was erected in the south aisle of the parish church
sometime in the 1930's. It bears the same fifty five names that are carved on the
town war memorial. Canon O. M. Jones (left) and W. W. (Bill) Sturley on the right.

One of the hymns sung at the dedication service was a recent addition to the Anglican Hymnary, 'The Supreme Sacrifice'. This newly-written hymn with words by J. S. Arkwright was being sung in Southam for the very first time. Its words would become very familiar and much loved by those who through the years would gather each Armisticetide round War Memorials up and down the land.

Those present on that cold December afternoon did not need to be reminded of those whose names they had come to commemorate. They had only to look around to be made painfully aware of the familiar faces now missing from the ranks of the church choir, the Town Band and the bell ringers. Practically every organisation represented at the service had been impoverished by the loss of colleagues killed in the war. Recently widowed wives contemplated the uncertain prospect of a future without a bread-winner. Many families had to come to terms with a father or son incapacitated by the war and for whom the future held out little save months or years of suffering and an early grave. For some their lives would be for ever blighted by the loss of sons and brothers who had barely reached adulthood.

In these days of political correctness and secular theology it is strange to learn that it is now looked upon as somehow slightly jingoistic and a bit 'infra dig' to commemorate the huge sacrifice made in the Great War by the singing of Arkwrights's hymn 'O Valiant Hearts' on Remembrance Sunday.

Eighty years on it is impossible to appreciate the extent to which everyone's lives were transfigured by the Great War. For some the changes were merely temporary, for others they were traumatic and permanent. Strange to think that a small Warwickshire town scarcely larger than many villages sent nearly 400 of its menfolk off to fight in what was in most respects someone else's war. All of the men are now long gone. The very least service that we can perform is to ensure that those 'valiant hearts' are never forgotten.

APPENDIX 1

THE NAMES ON THE WAR MEMORIAL

There is no surviving documentary evidence as to the manner in which the names which appear on the memorial were collated. What is known is that throughout the war there was pinned up in the Parish Church a Roll of Honour. Those who had lost loved ones in the war were asked to add their names to this list.

Prior to the finalising of the design of the memorial, a list of names which it was proposed to inscribe on it was placed in the window of Alfie Chambers the High Street printer and stationer. Any names that it was felt had been inadvertently omitted could be sent to the Rector who acted as chairman of the War Memorial Committee for inclusion on the memorial.

We do not know what criteria were adopted to determine which men qualified to have their names included on the war memorial. Some of those whose names appear were born in Southam and some were not. Some lived in the town whilst others had married and moved away. There is in the Congregational Church in Wood Street another memorial of the 1914 – 1918 war. This further complicates the whole subject since a number of the names on that memorial are not included on the town memorial. The chapel war memorial is dedicated to 'The men and boys of this church and Sunday School who made the supreme sacrifice in the Great war 1914 – 1918'. The criteria for inclusion on the Congregational Church tablet were thus membership of the church or Sunday School at some date. Such membership did not necessarily imply residence in Southam since people from many of the smaller villages in the district attended the Wood Street church.

What can be deduced with some degree of certainty is that it was residence in Southam for however brief a period that seemed to qualify men for inclusion on the town war memorial. There were a number of men who had worked in the town who were killed in the war but they seem to have been commemorated almost without exception in the places where they lived.

There are surprisingly some omissions. There can be little doubt that the Southam war memorial ought to include a number of names which are omitted. I can think of no reason why only one of the two Turner brothers who died is named on the memorial. Both were born in Southam and to the best of my knowledge lived in the town. Horace Parkinson's father had been Manager of Lloyds Bank in the High Street for many years and lived next to the Bank. Fred Constable had been born in the Union Workhouse and grew up in Southam as a lad and yet his name does not appear. Herbert Randall's father had been the resident landlord at the Bowling Green for many years.

The answer to these omissions lies I suspect in the attitude of the next-of-kin and their feelings about their loss at the time. In the case of Fred Constable there may not have been anyone sufficiently close to him or interested enough to ensure that his name was included. In the case of the Turner brothers there is no apparent reason. It might be that some of the families did not feel that they were sufficiently 'old Southam' to warrant inclusion.

I have tried to include in this work those who I feel have a legitimate claim to be called 'Southamites' either by virtue of birth or residence or simply because they were so regarded by other people in the town. I have included those men whose names are recorded on the Congregational Church memorial and one or two men whose names do not appear on either of the town's memorials.

What also became clear in the course of my research for this book is that a number of names have been incorrectly spelled both on the memorial and in the records held by the Commonwealth War Graves Commission at Maidenhead. Sometimes this fact was pointed out to me by surviving relatives, in other instances the Parish Registers have been cross-checked against names recorded by the CWGC and in the many volumes of *Soldiers Died* in the Birmingham Reference Library. To the best of my belief the names throughout the text and in the tables are the correct names. It will be seen that some are at variance with those on the war memorial.

I also discovered during the course of my research that the date of death of at least one of those killed had been incorrectly recorded in all of the official published sources that were consulted. William Baldwin's death has hitherto been recorded as having taken place in May 1916 but since local newspapers carried news of his death in its columns a year earlier, there can be no doubt that he was killed on May 10th 1915 and not in 1916. There are no doubt similar errors of transcription in the eighty or so volumes of *Soldiers Died*.

What may not be readily apparent to those who look at the Southam War Memorial today is the fact that in recent years new stone panels bearing the names of those commemorated have been fixed to the octagonal base of the memorial. The original incised names had become increasingly unreadable and it was decided that the memorial should be refurbished. There is one significant difference between the memorial as it stands today and when it was first erected in 1921. The original memorial displayed not only the names of the fallen but also their rank and the regiment or unit in which they were serving when they died.

The new panels which have been fixed to the memorial base on top of the original inscriptions bear only surnames and initials and none of the other details so helpful to local and family historians. These are now forever hidden from view. It was singularly unfortunate that before the refurbishment was carried out no one thought to record the details shown on the original memorial which were omitted as part of the restoration. Were it not for the fact that I managed to locate a copy of the Order of Service for the dedication of the memorial which contained the unit/regimental details this book would not have been possible.

PHOTO. DUHAMEEUW
MENIN GATE MEMORIAL. YPRES.

The Menin Gate memorial in Ypres was designed by Sir Reginal Bloomfield and bears the names of some fifty thousand British soldiers who died between 1914 and August 1917 and who have no known grave.

The huge Canadian Memorial on Vimy Ridge stands on what was Hill 145 and took eleven years to build. The Canadians had a reputation as formidable soldiers and 66,000 were killed in the war.

The Tyne Cot memorial and Cemetery marks the slope of Passchendale Ridge. Here lie the greatest number to be buried in any Commonwealth war cemetery anywhere in the world. There are 11,908 graves in this quiet and beautiful place. The memorial bears the names of 34,857 men who fell in the Ypres Salient and whose graves are unknown.

*The colonnade in the British Military Cemetery in Arras. The Arras Memorial
wall carries the names of 36,000 missing in the battles around Arras.
The cemetery contains 2,700 burials.*

*The Ploegsteert memorial guarded by British lions is unique in the Salient being the
only circular temple. The missing from many of the early Great War battles are listed
on the panels in the colonnade – in all 11,467 men.*

The Thiepval memorial to the Missing of the Somme battles records the names of over 73,000 men who have no known graves. The colossal arched memorial was designed by Sir Edward Lutyens. The Commonwealth War Graves Commission has a continuing programme of repairs to headstones and memorial panels. A CWGC stone mason is seen cutting names in a recently replaced panel on the memorial at Thiepval.

Bedford House Cemetery stands on the site of a moated chateau whose remains can still be seen in front of the cemetery. Bedford House is one of the largest cemeteries in the Salient and has plots of 1939 – 45 graves as well as those from 1914 – 18.

*Tom Worrall lies with other members of his gun team in
the tiny Track X cemetery near Sint Jan.*

*John Checkley the first Southam soldier to die in the war is buried with
other Royal Warwicks men in Strand Military Cemetery named after
'The Strand' a trench which led into Plugstreet Wood.*

115

William Garratt was killed just six weeks before the signing of the Armistice.
He is interred in Hooge Crater Cemetery along with two other Southam men.

John Bull one of the Southam emigrants was killed at Easter 1916
and is buried at Chester Farm Cemetery, Zillebeke.

APPENDIX 2

REGIMENTS/UNITS IN WHICH SOUTHAM MEN SERVED

Surname	First names	Rank	Army Number	Unit
Abbott	William	Private	10982	2nd South Staffs
Adams	Arthur	Private	18776	21st Manchester
Amos	William Thomas	Private	20900	1/6th Royal Warwicks
Askew	Harry Thomas	Rifleman	Z/903	1st Rifle Brigade
Baldwin	Frederick J	Gunner	11136	157 Bde R FA
Baldwin	Arthur Edward	Private	44205	2/4th Royal Berkshire
Baldwin	Charles Isaac	Sergeant		RASC
Baldwin	Harry	Driver	614277	2/1st(Warwick) RHA
Bicknell	Harry	Private	28034	10th Royal Warwicks
Bleloch	William Alison	L/Cpl	285033	Oxfordshire Yeomanry
Brain	William Harry	Sergeant	9009	1st Royal Welsh Fusiliers
Bull	George Riley	Sergeant	11459	4th Canadian Infantry
Bull	John Edward	Private	11329	4th Canadian Infantry
Burnell	William Charles	Private	1884	2nd Royal Warwicks
Carter	Leonard Bertie	Private	402480	10th Canadian Infantry
Checkley	John	Private	9671	1st Royal Warwicks
Collier	William Charles	Private	202908	16th Royal Warwicks
Constable	Frederick William	Private	18366	6th Northamptonshire
Court	Frederick William	Ch.Armourer	340995(C)	Royal Navy
Davenport	Ernest Edward	Actg Corporal	9708	2nd Royal Welsh Fusiliers
Davidson	William Thomas C	Captain		1st Dorsetshire
Devenport	Alfred William	Gunner	39449	108th Heavy Bty RGA
Devenport	Arthur John	Private	21118	6th Leicestershire
Duckett	Arthur John	Private	28809	11th Royal Warwicks
Duckett	John	Private	9011	2nd Royal Welsh Fusiliers

Fennell	Alfred Edwin	Private	281678	Labour Corps
Fennell	Joseph Henry	Private	437203	RAMC
Flowers	Percy Preston	Private	51164	1/6th West Yorkshire
Flowers	Harry	Private	34980	5th Royal Berkshire
Garratt	William George	Private	139349	9th Bn Machine Gun Corps
Gillmore	David Henry	L/Cpl	18893	16th Royal Warwicks
Glenn	Henry	Private	202898	2/7th Royal Warwicks
Gould	William	L/Cpl	26616	2nd Rifle Brigade
Griffin	Ralph	Private	7517	1st Bedfordshire
Hancocks	William Frederick	Private	19549	1st Coldstream Guards
Hancox	Frank Louis	Private	19338	10th Royal Warwicks
Harrison	Allen	Private	10178	8th Royal Fusiliers
Hart-Davies	Ivan Beauclerk	Lt		35Tr. Squadron RFC
Hartley	Frederick George	Corporal	13833	19th Bn Machine Gun Corps
Hincks	Edward Warner	L/Cpl	G/11127	11th Middlesex
Hollis	Ernest Joseph	Private	35959	3rd Worcestershire
Hughes	Sidney	Driver	T4/185219	RASC
King	John Henry Lake	Gunner	614505	2/1st (Warwick) RHA
Lattey	Alexander Davidson	Midshipman	228	Royal Navy
Lee	Bernard George	Lt		180 Bde RFA
Masters	Thomas	Fitter Staff Sgt	955287	236 Bde RFA
Morby	Henry Thomas	Private	18404	2nd Gloucestershire
Morgan	Albert	Private	33634	8th Gloucestershire
Owen	Ernest Clinch	L/Cpl	439134	52nd Canadian Infantry
Parkinson	Horace James Ankers	2nd Lt		4th Leicestershire
Pearson	Hubert Reeve	Sapper	32962	82nd Field Coy RE
Pittom	William Richard	Private	5500	2/5th Royal Warwicks
Pratt	Ernest Alfred	Private	6306	1/14th London Scottish
Pratt	Ernest Arthur	Private	306800	1/8th Royal Warwicks
Randall	Herbert Henry	Ldg Seaman	204195	Royal Navy
Rathbone	Arthur James	Private	27991	1st Royal Warwicks
Rockingham	Thomas	Private	28588	15th Royal Warwicks
Seckington	William Harold	Private	G/7031	11th Queens Royal
Shearsby	Edmund Thomas	Private	21711 12th	Gloucestershire
Shorthouse	George Henry	Trooper	1868	Warwickshire Yeomanry
Smith	William Alfred	Private	17185	4th Grenadier Guards
Turner	Arthur Charles	Private	201775	2/7th Royal Warwicks
Turner	Edward Walter	Private	TF/241270	1st Queens Own (RWK)
Wellings	Edwin	Private	1959	2nd Royal Warwicks
Worrall	Thomas	Gunner	614503	2/1st(Warwick) RHA

APPENDIX 3

PLACE OF BURIAL/COMMEMORATION

Surname	Initials	Date Of Death	Grave/memorial
Abbott	W.	13.11.16	Thiepval Memorial
Adams	A.	01.07.16	Thiepval Memorial
Amos	W. T.	04.02.17	Assevillers New British Cemetery
Askew	H. T.	27.04.15	Menin Gate
Baldwin	F. J.	04.12.17	Solferino Farm Cemetery
Baldwin	A. E.	13.09.18	Laventie Military Cemetery
Baldwin	C. I.	31.12.20	Southam Churchyard
Baldwin	H.	15.10.17	Duhallow ADS Cemetery
Bicknell	H.	16.06.18	Dendermonde Communal Cemetery Extension
Bleloch	W. A.	01.07.17	Templeux-le-Guerard British Cemetery
Brain	W. H.	25.09.15	Loos Memorial
Bull	G. R.	08.08.18	Caix British Cemetery
Bull	J. E.	10.04.16	Chester Farm Cemetery, Zillebeke
Burnell	W. C.	16.05.15	Thiepval Memorial
Carter	L. B.	09.04.17	Nine Elms Cemetery, Thelus
Checkley	J.	27.10.14	Strand Military Cemetery
Collier	W. C.	09.10.17	Hooge Crater Cemetery
Constable	F. W.	14.07.16	Thiepval Memorial
Court	F. W.	22.09.14	Royal Navy Memorial Chatham
Davenport	E. E.	29.04.15	Bois Grenier Communal Cemetery
Davidson	W. T. C.	13.10.14	Le Touret Memorial, Pas de Calais
Devenport	A. W.	07.07.16	Etaples Military Cemetery
Devenport	A. J.	17.07.16	Thiepval Memorial
Duckett	A. J.	09.10.17	Voormezele Enclosures
Duckett	J.	21.10.18	Southam churchyard
Fennell	A. E.	30.03.18	Southam churchyard
Fennell	J. H.	28.12.17	Padua Main Cemetery, Italy

Flowers	P. P.	12.02.18	Menin Road South Military Cemetery, Ypres
Flowers	H.	28.04.17	Arras Memorial
Garratt	W. G.	28.09.18	Hooge Crater Cemetery
Gillmore	D. H.	12.05.17	Barlin Communal Cemetery Extension Pas de Calais
Glenn	H.	28.12.17	Abbeville Communal Cemetery Extension
Gould	W.	12.11.16	Thiepval Memorial
Griffin	R.	08.01.15	Menin Gate
Hancocks	W. F.	21.09.17	Tyne Cot Memorial
Hancox	F. L.	05.06.18	La Cheppe French National Cemetery
Harrison	A.	01.05.17	Happy Valley British Cemetery, Fampoux
Hart-Davies	I. B.	27.07.17	Southam churchyard
Hartley	F. G.	13.09.19	Murmansk British Cemetery, Russia
Hincks	E. W.	12.04.17	Feuchy Chapel British Cemetery, Wancourt
Hollis	E. J.	22.03.18	Arras Memorial, Pas de Calais
Hughes	S.	03.02.18	Southam churchyard
King	J. H. L.	08.08.17	New Irish Farm Cemetery
Lattey	A. D.	15.10.14	Royal Navy Memorial Chatham
Lee	B. G.	22.03.18	Roye New British Cemetery
Masters	T.	02.06.17	Bedford House Cemetery
Morby	H. T.	02.10.16	Struma Military Cemetery, Greece
Morgan	A.	10.11.17	Outtersteene Communal Cemetery Extension
Owen	E. C.	20.06.16	Menin Gate
Parkinson	H. J. A.	01.07.17	Clifton Road Cemetery, Rugby
Pearson	H. R.	14.01.16	Merville Communal Cemetery
Pittom	W. R.	02.07.16	Rue-Du-Bacquerot Military Cemetery
Pratt	E. Alfred	01.07.16	Thiepval Memorial
Pratt	E. Arthur	27.08.16	Thiepval Memorial
Randall	H. H.	12.03.17	Royal Navy Memorial, Portsmouth
Rathbone	A. J.	15.04.18	Ploegsteert Memorial
Rockingham	T	30.06.18	Ploegsteert Memorial
Seckington	W. H.	13.08.18	Esquelbec Military Cemetery
Shearsby	E. T.	25.08.18	Queen's Cemetery, Pas de Calais
Shorthouse	G. H.	29.11.20	Carlby churchyard Lincolnshire
Smith	W. A.	16.11.16	Grove Town Cemetery, Meaulte
Turner	A. C.	28.02.19	Etaples Military Cemetery
Turner	E. W.	26.10.17	Hooge Crater Cemetery
Wellings	E.	19.12.14	Ploegsteert Memorial
Worrall	T.	16.08.17	Track 'X' Cemetery

INDEX